Acknowledgements

THE IDEA FOR THIS BOOK would never have been turned into a reality without the enthusiastic support of our friend and colleague, demographer David Baxter and the staff of the Urban Futures Institute in Vancouver. David generously guided us to the information we needed to document the demographic trends underlying many of the major social and public policy issues of our time. The Urban Futures Institute is an important source of demographic data and analysis for the entire country.

Dennis Wong of Statistics Canada's office in Vancouver has been an invaluable guide to their voluminous publications. Canadians are fortunate that our national statistical agency is one of the best in the world. We have been fortunate in the cheerful and constructive assistance provided by Dennis.

Jenica Neamu, a recent graduate of the University of British Columbia's School of Library, Archival and Information Studies, has been our indefatigable research assistant on this project; she demonstrated conclusively that when you need to find information, you should seek the assistance of a librarian. She is the compiler of the Appendix of Internet resources and we appreciate her work more than we can say.

We were alerted to important legal issues in the area of mandatory retirement by lawyer Kathleen A. Archibald and appreciate her willingness to share with us her unpublished paper on the subject.

We are blessed with friends who have shown a great interest in our project and made helpful suggestions: Dennis Bergson, Cec Brown, Wally Craver, Bruce and Inta Hasenkamp, John Hobday, Suzanne Labarge, Heidi and Ray Peters, John Watson, and Wendy and Brian White.

We would like to express our gratitude to the fascinating "retired" individuals who were kind enough to share their personal stories with us for the profiles in this book. These delightful people made our task both enjoyable and interesting. They are (in alphabetical order): Tom Brown, Shaun Butler, Joy Coghill, Ken Fiddes, Jim Gray, Margaret Labarge, Peter Lougheed, Tom McCabe, Doreen McKenzie-Sanders, Sylvia Ostry, Paddy Sherman, Gordon Watson, and Alcid and George Yelle.

Thanks also go to our calm and constructive editor, Brian Scrivener, as well as to John Eerkes-Medrano for meticulous copy-editing and Robin Van Heck for careful proofreading. The visionary folks at Douglas & McIntyre have been a joy to work with: Scott McIntyre, Susan Rana, Peter Cocking, Val Speidel and Kym Lyons.

David Bond &
Diane **Bond**

Future Perfect

RETIREMENT STRATEGIES FOR PRODUCTIVE **PEOPLE**

Douglas & McIntyre
Vancouver/Toronto

02 03 04 05 06 5 4 3 2 1

Douglas & McIntyre
2323 Quebec Street, Suite 201
Vancouver, British Columbia
V5T 4S7
www.douglas-mcintyre.com

National Library of Canada Cataloguing in Publication Data

Bond, David E.

Future perfect : retirement strategies for productive people / David Bond and Diane Bond.

Includes bibliographical references.

ISBN 1-55054-957-X

1. Retirement—Planning. I. Bond, Diane, 1949– II. Title.

HQ1062.B64 2003 646.7'9 C2002-911258-3

Editing by Brian Scrivener
Cover design by Peter Cocking
Text design by Val Speidel
Printed and bound in Canada by Friesens
Printed on acid-free paper ∞

The publisher gratefully acknowledges the financial support of the Canada Council for the Arts, the British Columbia Ministry of Tourism, Small Business and Culture, and the Government of Canada through the Book Publishing Industry Development Program (BPIDP) for our publishing activities.

Contents

Introduction

PLANNING FOR RETIREMENT has always been a popular topic for discussion at our house. We married rather late in life (Diane was 45 and David was 57), and David was already happily crossing off the days to retirement from his position as a bank economist, due in April 1998 with his 60th birthday. Diane was launching a small business and was already looking forward to the day when it would no longer require her daily hands-on management.

Of course, we talked about our financial plan and worked closely with a financial planner to make decisions about David's pension options and our personal investment programs. But we found making our plans for what we wanted to *do* in future even more absorbing. David was looking forward to a reprise of his early career as a university professor and developing a public-speaking profile. Diane planned to take a step back from the day-to-day pressures of running a business to incorporate time for consulting and writing projects. Most of all, we looked forward to working together on a project. Many ideas were tried on for size, but writing this book was the one that held our interest.

On a personal level, we began to realize that a traditional retirement had no place in our plans. Neither of us could imagine going from the fast lane one day to watching the soaps the next. Our financial planning was not targeted to releasing us from wage slavery but to allowing us to choose—choose where we would live, when and for whom we would work and what non-career interests we would pursue.

As avid readers, we observed that a great deal has been written and spoken about the financial side of planning for retirement. Given increasing life expectancies, this is a very good thing! But, we noted, there was relatively little public discussion about preparing to answer the question: What will I do with the 2,500 hours a year I used to dedicate to my employer, my business or my clients—and to the joys of commuting?

While we were noodling about the best way to achieve contentment and fulfillment in our "golden" years, the demographers and economists were crunching numbers. They were preparing reports predicting that the aging of the baby boom generation will overwhelm our health care system, bankrupt the Canada Pension Plan and leave organizations of all kinds unable to find enough workers to replace their new retirees. The first whispers reached us in a 1996 *Atlantic Monthly* article by Peter Peterson. The investment banker cum social commentator warned of the demographic hurdles facing the U.S. social security system in the early 21st century. As a baby boomer, Diane was immediately fascinated—and worried that she would end up being a member of the most disliked generation in history. As an economist and former federal bureaucrat, David began thinking through the labour market and public policy fallout.

Within just a few years, the whisper had become a constant roar. We began to hear about the "retirement crisis." In July 1999, Canadian demographer David Baxter predicted in a paper entitled "Help Wanted" that "Canada will have a labour shortage within a decade." The lead article in *The Economist* of September 4, 1999, was headed "Let Old Folk Work."

At about the same time that the doomsayers began to work up a real head of steam, the American Association of Retired Persons let it be known that in the future AARP would not be an acronym but the association's full name. Market research had uncovered an amazing fact: large numbers of Americans turning 50—AARP's target market for the recruitment of new members—are not planning to retire, at least not in the conventional sense of the term.

In the face of these developments, we concluded that what had begun as a discussion about personal fulfillment should grow to include an examination of the major forces in our society that were remaking retirement.

The macro trends make very interesting and sometimes sobering reading. It's important to be aware of them, because they will eventually revolutionize government policies affecting retirement age and retirement income. They will also eventually change profoundly the relationships between employer and employee, between the seller and the buyer of labour—including your labour! And they will change how you invest for and plan for a retirement that may be very different from that of your parents' generation.

We began to collect the stories of individuals for whom retirement was a transition to another work style. There was the limosine driver David met one day on his way to the airport in Toronto. Being naturally chatty, David asked him how long he had been driving the limo. "About three months," was the reply. "And what did you do before?" It turned out the limo driver was a retired vice-president of General Electric who had become seriously bored and whose wife insisted he find something to do. As she said, "I married you for better or for worse, but not for lunch." Reasoning that he enjoyed meeting people and driving, he approached the airport limousine companies and was soon getting to know Toronto better than he had in his entire life. He had reinvented himself in a new role of his own choosing.

We also observed this phenomenon at an individual level among our friends and associates. Many who had passed the traditional retirement age had not stepped aside but rather struck out on new paths. They spoke of renewal, not retirement. Some of them appear later in this book as case studies. On the other hand, some of our younger acquaintances looked ahead to a planned retirement date with fear and loathing. They could not imagine what they would do. Several said, "We hope you really write this book because we really need to prepare for this." Well, we really wrote the book. We hope it helps!

Of course, many other writers, researchers and organizations have recognized the need for easily-available information to help people live productive, healthy and interesting lives in their

50s, 60s and beyond. There is a wealth of information accessible via the Internet. This book includes as an Appendix an annotated listing of about 100 Web sites covering such broad interest areas as learning and skills development, volunteering, business and career, and living well. We hope some of these sites will be added to each reader's personal list of bookmarks.

Chapter 1

Exploding the Retirement Myths

SINCE VERY FEW OF US have taken a formal course in planning for retirement, many of us accept the popular myths about retirement that are rapidly being superseded by the social, demographic and economic realities of the new millennium. Things have changed a lot since your parents retired—in fact, we believe traditional retirement is fast going out of style.

Before looking at the "new" retirement, let's haul out these myths and take a good look at them.

Myth #1

Your life in retirement will be short; planning to play golf every day is all the plan you need.

> **In fact, your retirement will likely be 15, 25 or even 35 years; you'll have more time than you need to whittle away at your handicap.**

When retirement was invented in Europe in the late 19th century, life expectancy was much shorter than it is today in the Western democracies. In 1935, when Franklin D. Roosevelt created social security in the United States, a man of 65 could expect to live an average of three years in retirement. Today, a 65-year-old Canadian male can expect to see his 81st birthday and a 65-year-old female will likely live past her 85th birthday. Further, the chances of serious disability among the "young old" (up to 75) are much reduced.

These improvements are the result of better nutrition and a greater consciousness of the importance of a healthy lifestyle in large segments of the population—as well as the quantum leaps made by medicine in the last 75 years. Think of the amazing advances made in the 20th century: the discovery of insulin in 1921–22 and penicillin in 1928—though first used in 1941—and later other powerful antibiotics; the advances in workplace safety; open heart surgery; the improvement in cancer survival rates from chemotherapy and nuclear medicine. Canadians born in 1951 had at birth an expectation of an average lifespan of 68.5 years, compared with the 49 years their grandparents born in 1901 could expect. Those of the 1951 cohort who celebrated the new millennium in 2000 could expect to live 30 or more years into that millennium.

Demographers also believe these estimates may be conservative. This is because the projections do not take account of the further gains in longevity that are almost certain to come as medical knowledge progresses and as we all work on maintaining fitness levels. And so, demographers advise those of us who are old enough to be thinking about retirement that we should plan to reach 90 years of age.

THERE IS LIFE AFTER POLITICS: PETER LOUGHEED

Peter Lougheed, a former premier of Alberta, does not like the word "retirement." He uses the vocabulary of change and renewal to describe his preparation for his "next career"—a preparation that began early in his second term as premier. As he says, "After two terms you begin to defend the record, and that's the time to go."

Peter was 56 when his career in elected office came to an end in 1985, and he considered conventional retirement not to be a possibility. To him, "retirement" meant inactivity, and that was the last thing he wanted. He wanted change. He had observed that many people, when they retire, become boring, and he did not want this to happen to him.

Peter does not believe in leaving things to chance. He likes to be in control of events that may have an impact on him. It's not surprising, therefore, that he approached his transition in a very organized and deliberate way. He started by asking himself one simple, central question: "What can I do that will be interesting and stimulating in the next phase in my life?"

He eliminated several options early on. He knew he did not want to return to practising law full time. He also decided that he did not want to run a business. Further, he hoped that whatever he did would be on the national stage and not the local or provincial one. He also knew that he did not want to be working on his own. He had been a team player and group leader for too long to forgo the human contact of working with others daily. A role that filled all these "negative requirements" was found in a Calgary law firm as counsel rather than as an active partner.

Peter began while still premier to make an inventory of his non-legal skills, such as chairing a meeting, reading briefing books and asking penetrating questions, all of which had served him well in his political career. As he developed that inventory he talked it over with several close and long-time friends whom he knew would give him the "straight goods."

Those friends remarked that the skills he had developed in politics would serve him well in the role of a corporate director and helped him put his name forward as a possible board member. Also, when travelling to Ontario and Quebec, he "networked" with business people he knew might be able to help him gain board appointments.

During his first 18 months after leaving office, he gained appointments mainly with national companies that had most, if not all, of their operations outside Alberta. He found that having a range of board appointments gave him a great deal of independence in asking hard questions of management, which he believes made him a more effective and valuable director.

Peter's political contacts brought some interesting international assignments, such as co-chair of the United States–Canada Free Trade Committee—intense assignments for limited periods of time, which he estimates have taken 10 per cent of his efforts since leaving office.

With the combination of acting as an adviser at a law firm, corporate directorships and carefully chosen volunteer assignments, Peter found a balance that worked for him. He continued, however, to keep his eye on the future. Knowing that once he reached the age of 70 he would be forced to give up his role on many boards, he became the chancellor of Queen's University in 1995—just after undergoing heart bypass surgery. He filled this rewarding role through 2002. In recognition of the passing years, he also looked forward to more time for travel and leisure activities with his wife, Jeanne, and his friends.

When asked what he would advise others to do, he recommends planning early—well before the usual retirement age. He is skeptical about asking friends for their advice. "They will want you to do just what they did," he says with a laugh. "They want you to affirm that they did the right thing. It may be right for them, but that does not mean it is right for you."

He cautions that there is a widely held myth about retirement: that it will be a little foretaste of heaven with endless freedom, great pleasure and few responsibilities. "Men, particularly, underestimate their need for consuming interests and activities after retirement, and their wives, long used to pursuing their own interests while their spouse pursued a career, may not anticipate this need on their spouse's behalf." The answer, he believes, is to gain the self-knowledge necessary to know what it is that will make *you* happy, and not to just accept the myth uncritically.

Peter believes it is extremely important to make an honest inventory of your skills and perform a reality check with people whose judgement you can rely upon. Then start thinking where those skills can be best used in a way that will allow you to make a contribution and will provide you with pleasure. Next, make efforts to generate opportunities to do those things that you believe will give you the greatest satisfaction.

He also recommends that if you chose to embark on a new career in which you hope to earn income, you make your financial expectations modest and budget accordingly. In this way, you will be able to judge your success by the intangible rewards of your work—and if you exceed your financial goals, that's a bonus. Finally, he advises, "Strike the word 'retirement' from your lexicon."

Peter Lougheed's experience points out a few home truths that business people will recognize as principles for the good management of any venture, be it a career or a company:

- Accept the inevitability of change, and love it if you possibly can.
- Planning means generating real options and evaluating them. This is an important and very concrete activity that should take a good amount of time and energy.
- Achieving self-knowledge is not the easiest thing for most of us, and we should not be afraid to ask for help.

Here's the key question. If you are 49 years old and expect to retire at 60, are you really excited about the prospect of playing golf for 20 or 30 years? If you are, and if you are confident that your savings and pensions will see you through to 100 (to be on the safe side), you may not need to read any more of this book. Maybe you should pass it on to a friend who doesn't play golf.

Myth #2

You are washed up at 65, or even 55; you have nothing left to contribute and your "best before" date is definitely history.

> **The fact of the matter is that older workers have advantages in some areas.**

This is the most pernicious of the retirement myths, because we are all secretly afraid it may be true. What corporate high flier of 55 hasn't looked at his 35-year-old second in command and wondered if she wasn't just a little too keen to take over and watch the former mentor slip into honourable but out-of-the-way retirement? What 50-year-old self-employed business-woman hasn't asked herself if having misplaced the car keys yet again might indicate premature dementia and not just the temporary short-term memory loss that often accompanies menopause?

There are some occupations in which youth and physical

vigour are clearly related to job performance. We don't send 60-year-olds to fight wars, and we probably don't want to fly on a 747 piloted by a heart-attack survivor. There's also the undeniable fact that for most of us endurance decreases with age. The 45-year-old senior partner in a large law firm recalls that as a young articling student, he could research legal precedents till midnight and still show up at the office by 8 A.M. ready to attack the next file. Now he finds that he needs a regular recovery time to give his clients the kind of quality advice they expect. He should also remember that the advice his clients pay so handsomely for is largely the product of 20 years' experience.

ALL THE WORLD'S A STAGE: JOY COGHILL

Joy Coghill is a theatre person. She was the driving force behind Vancouver's Holiday Theatre, the first professional children's theatre in Canada. She became the artistic director of the Vancouver Playhouse and later taught in the National Theatre School.

In her years in the theatre, Joy developed many skills, from acting to producing. Her acting extended beyond the stage to films, television and radio. In short, she is a consummate thespian. She claims there was no design to her career, that one thing just led to another, but along the way she was learning and taking joy in the creative process. She developed an infectious passion for living life to the fullest.

Even Joy's entry into the world of theatre was not planned. After graduating from the University of British

Columbia, she planned to do graduate work in stage direction in Chicago. But she found it deadly dull and was ready to pack her bags and return to Vancouver when she met Charlotte Chorpenning, a woman in her 80s who, in Joy's words, "came bouncing down the hall." Charlotte was the founder of the first professional children's theatre in the United States. Joy was hooked, and she devoted the first "act" of her career to children's theatre. To this day, Joy believes theatre is a wonderful method of teaching and conveying both ideas and values to children.

Joy never thought about retiring. Though she herself always found increasing opportunities to work, she knew full well that as actors age the demand for their services declines. Perversely, as an actor becomes more practised in his or her craft, the demand for such experience falls off. So Joy came up with the idea for Golden West, a theatre company for actors over the age of 60, the first such organization in the world. She conceived of it as a vehicle to provide a showcase for older actors to demonstrate to themselves and to the public that they had something to offer—that their skills and craftsmanship were worth seeing.

Joy raised the necessary funds, selected the plays and hired actors—in fact, she presided over every detail. The result has been a unique theatrical experience for both players and audience. The beneficiaries are not just the players but those in the audience, who are invited to re-evaluate their preconceptions about what is possible for professionals of traditional retirement age to achieve.

But while it had been possible for Joy to maintain a breakneck pace indefinitely 30 years earlier, the stress of starting up Golden West started to affect her health. In 1998, she had to undergo heart surgery. Then, as she says, "I had to get rid of the stress or I would die. The hard part was that I was brought up to believe that you only let something go when it was in excellent shape, not when it was struggling to survive." She asked three friends if any one of them would take over the project. They agreed to work together and take over her responsibilities.

Stepping back was not something Joy did easily. "I thrived on stress. I thought it was essential to life, and here I was being told to get rid of it—all of it—or I would die." She turned to pottery, something she had never done before, taking a course at the Emily Carr Institute of Art & Design. She found it entrancing, especially the creative aspects of form and decoration. This new creative experience allowed her to bridge the age chasm and share her excitement and enthusiasm with her much younger classmates.

Of late, Joy has taken on another project: helping to establish a retirement home for actors in Vancouver. She still acts in films but only works with people she likes, and does so for only half a day at a time. In 2002, she received the Governor General's Award for lifetime achievement in the arts.

Joy believes that after 60 you get out of life what you put into it. "You just can't sit around idle. That is what hastens your departure, and why leave life early, when it is so full of varied and interesting and exciting challenges? If you don't live, you die.

"What someone should do well before the time of retirement is to discover those things which give them special pleasure and then see how those pleasures can become more numerous. Shed the dull parts and concentrate on the creative parts. You have to take the God-given energy that you have trained and honed throughout your life and apply it where it is needed. You can apply it to gardening or volunteer work or mentoring or whatever, but it must be used and, in using it, you gain from life. You have to be creating something and making a contribution.

"I don't really trust the word 'youth.' I think it is not all that wonderful. The experience, the wisdom you gain from living is what really counts, and that wisdom is only maximized if you live life passionately. That is what we should all strive to do. Just because you have reached a certain age is no reason to stop living. What you need to do is to get involved in something that challenges your total self—something that gives you a wow. But then I am an artist, and I so enjoy life."

There are some lessons to be learned here.

- Sometimes our life's great enthusiasm finds us by accident, as children's theatre found Joy. Whether we are 25 or 65, the great trick is to be open to new possibilities and not to dismiss them when they come along as deviating too far from the path that we have set out for ourselves.

- Just because something has not been done before is not proof that it cannot or should not be done. There was really no reason why an acting troupe of over-60s couldn't perform convincingly and compellingly—so Joy just did it.
- The increased demands of looking after one's health are an inevitable part of aging, but we can learn to take satisfaction in accomplishing things through others, as well as in what we ourselves contribute.

This myth of the "best before" date ignores the increasingly obvious fact that few careers now are linear and that most of us do different jobs at different times in our lives. Consciously or unconsciously, we select roles for which we are suited at the time. A woman who has laboured hard physically for decades raising children and working as a professional nurse may, in her 40s or 50s, turn to a job in sales or customer service that uses her well-honed people skills but does not require the same degree of physical effort. A man who has climbed the corporate ladder in a hard-driving finance or marketing function may decide, once the children are educated and the mortgage paid down, to take himself out of the fray and become a business adviser or hands-on investor or even something quite different.[1]

Myth #3

You have to step aside to create opportunities for the younger generation.

In fact, the younger generation needs you to keep working and paying your taxes!

How many times have you heard a 50- or 60-something talk about stepping aside to give the young people a chance? The tone is usually somewhat self-congratulatory and has a barely detectable undercurrent of "If I say this often enough, I'll eventually really believe it." Well, we can all stop trying to believe it, because the best thing we can do for our children and grandchildren is to stay productive, keep paying taxes and continue contributing to their RESPs.

Where on earth did this dopey "step-aside" idea come from? It originates in the widely disseminated—but utterly fallacious—"lump of labour" theory.[2] This theory says that there is just so much work to go around and that anyone who holds two jobs, logs overtime or continues work after 55 is depriving some other person of gainful employment. In the case of the reluctant retiree, he or she is portrayed as preventing a younger worker with kids to feed and a house down-payment to save from getting a firm footing on a good career path. Unions are often staunch supporters of this theory, believing that the easiest way they can acquire more members is for older workers to retire early so that their jobs can be taken over by apprentices.

In recent years, the notion has gained credibility because there has been a labour surplus in North America ever since the baby boomers entered the workforce beginning in the mid-1960s. Those of us who are now 35 to 55 have faced strong competition for the "good" jobs all our working lives because there are so many of us. Those of us who are 55 to 65 may have been on the receiving end of not-so-subtle hints that we should give up the corner office to a young Gen-X turk. After all, the youngster has cut his teeth on hard drives and has had to clamour up the ladder of responsibility through layers of baby boomers like so much jungle undergrowth.

Figure 1: **POPULATION BY AGE AND SEX, CANADA, 2000**

source: Urban Futures Institute

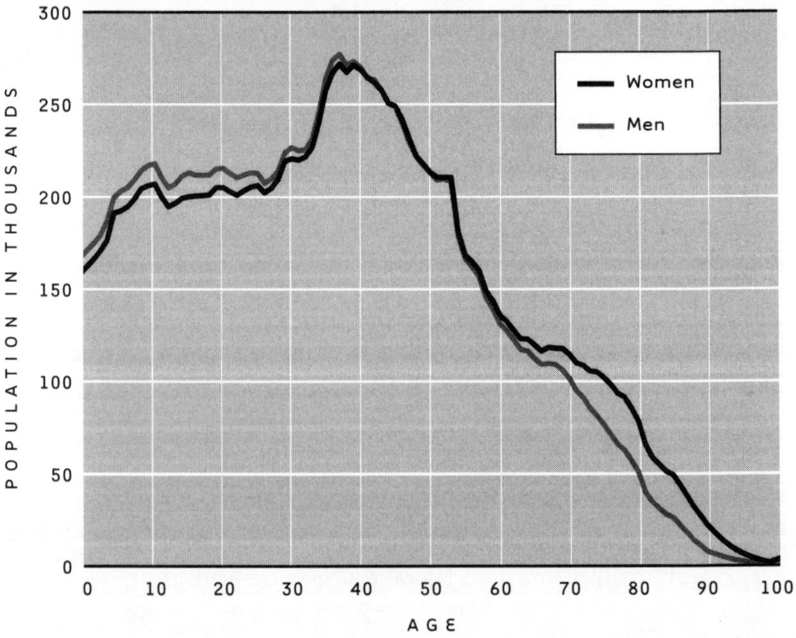

All this is about to change. When the baby boomers start retiring in significant numbers in a few years' time, finding replacements is not going to be all that easy. As shown in Figure 1, the age cohorts following after the baby boomers are substantially smaller in number. Already recruiters are finding that there are not as many 35- to 45-year-olds who want to try for the very top jobs as there were only a few years ago. In 2004, all the baby boomers will be over 40, and many will have discovered that they want more out of life than endless business travel or 60-hour work weeks. The buyers' market will—quite rapidly—become a sellers' market.[3]

Myth #4

You can never learn new skills after age 50 or 55, so you won't be able to keep up in the knowledge-based economy.

> **In fact, you can continue to learn throughout your life—as long as you develop and maintain your learning skills.**

"Lifelong learning" is one of those public-service-announcement phrases used so often that it no longer registers on the consciousness. When it began to be clear in the 1980s that career-long employment with one company or even one industry was no longer a realistic expectation for most workers, the virtues of training and retraining were touted loudly. Governments, educational institutions and private-sector firms rushed to offer programs to turn fishers into eco-tour guides and displaced middle managers into entrepreneurs. Then came the cries of anguish from trainees who complained they were trained for jobs that don't exist and from would-be entrepreneurs who discovered there is a lot more to starting your own business than taking a marketing course. Perhaps the public can be forgiven if it became a little cynical about "training programs."

But don't become cynical about the importance of learning at all stages in our lives. Like eating and sleeping, learning is a necessary human activity. The love of learning turns necessity into pleasure, just as loving fine food can turn meeting the need for daily sustenance into a recurring source of enjoyment. If you have been fortunate enough to form the habits of staying informed, reading widely and discussing ideas with others, you probably love to learn, and the increasing number of candles on the birthday cake is not going to stop you.

OLD DOG LEARNS NEW TRICKS: GORDON WATSON

Gordon Watson has been an archaeologist for more than 25 years—ever since he retired from the public service of Canada in 1975. And at 84 years of age, he's still going strong. He is currently supervising a major dig in eastern Ontario that he believes will require as much as 30 more years' work to complete.

As a young boy growing up on a farm in Saskatchewan,

Gordon found all sorts of aboriginal artifacts as his father broke the sod on their farm. He believes that those finds were the first sparks to light his interest in archaeology. As an undergraduate at the University of Western Ontario, however, he studied physics, a subject that would open doors to more career options than would archaeology. Back in 1940, straight out of university, he joined the army, but because of his training in sciences he was diverted into a research role—something he did for 35 years. His interest in archaeology was revived, however, in the early 1970s, as he was approaching the time when he could retire from the public service without sacrificing any pension income.

Gordon and his wife, Margaret, had a cottage along the Ottawa River, and in the summer of 1970 they brought in a bulldozer to prepare a site for some construction. When he and his family were raking over the cleared site, they found numerous pottery shards.

Gordon's first thought was to inform the professional archaeologist at the National Museum of Man in Ottawa (now the Canadian Museum of Civilization in Hull) of his find and to ask if the museum would be interested in digging on the site before it was covered with cement. "No," was the reply. "The museum staff is mandated to dig only on public lands." The museum was willing to give him some reading material on archaeological techniques, but he would be on his own if he wanted to actually dig up anything. So dig he did. For four years, he uncovered a host of artifacts on the site, all of which he carefully catalogued.

Gordon joined a group of professionals and amateurs in the Ottawa chapter of the Canadian Archaeological Society and began to think he needed some formal training in the science. In part, his pursuit of further education was motivated by the Ontario government's decision to require anyone supervising an archaeological dig to have a licence. The licences would only be issued to qualified professionals.

In the fall of 1975, Gordon enrolled in the masters of arts program in archaeology at Trent University. He received his M.A. in 1980. His master's thesis involved a field study of what became known as the White site, so named after the person on whose property the site was located. Mr. White approached Gordon after a public lecture and asked whether he might identify some artifacts found near the White home. When Gordon got to the site, which would occupy him for more than four years, the White children were kicking up pottery shards as they dragged their feet along the ground from their swing. This turned out to be an important find, showing that human settlement had occurred in the Rideau River and lake system around 6000 B.C.

The White dig led to others, and for the next 20 years Gordon was busy collecting material from a host of sites throughout Ontario. In 1997, he decided that perhaps it was time to retire from this second—albeit unpaid—career, so he donated more than 70,000 artifacts to the Canadian

Museum of Civilization. However, at an "Archaeology Day" at a nearby provincial park, one of park officials came over with a box full of artifacts and asked Gordon if he could identify them. Indeed, he could. The result was another significant find, dating back as far as 10,000 B.C. Soon the 70,000 artifacts that had been donated to the museum were replaced by another 70,000 unearthed at the new dig. Gordon's son recently recounted that, when he visits his parents, the dining room table is covered with material and that the bedrooms he and his brother once slept in are packed with pieces of the new collection.

For more than 30 years, Gordon Watson has enjoyed a second career as a not-so-amateur archaeologist happily engaged in the pursuit of intellectual goals. Archaeology, as he said, really consists of solving puzzles. How did these ancient people live? What were their lives like? Why did they occupy this particular site? What changes were going on around them, and how well did they adapt?

In trying to solve those puzzles, Gordon has found something to challenge his mind and fill his days with meaningful work that he enjoys and that brings him recognition for real contributions to his field. To say that his has been a successful retirement is to understate the case. As he approached retirement from his first career, Gordon rediscovered, almost by accident, a boyhood interest. Then he pursued it with both discipline and passionate interest—and with an adventurousness of spirit that brought him many opportunities to use his increasing expertise.

What can be learned from this wonderful story of a perfectly realized second career?

- Becoming an accomplished amateur (literally, one who pursues an occupation out of love rather than for material gain) can be extremely rewarding.
- Although a second career may offer an opportunity to fulfill a long-cherished dream, it may also require serious study and preparation—just like a first career.
- The support and understanding of those closest to you are as important as your own commitment to your venture. If your dream is going to occupy the dining room table and fill the kids' rooms, it's best if your spouse and children share—or at least empathize with—your enthusiasm.

What does change with age is the relative ease of various kinds of learning. Learning to speak a new language can be difficult because distinguishing tonality might be more difficult if there has been some hearing loss, but learning to read it and write it should be no problem just because of age. There are countless stories about seniors learning to surf the Web and do rather sophisticated computer work. If you have been learning all your life—it's called gaining experience—then learning in a more formal setting may take some getting used to, but your mental capacities should be acute.[4]

Myth #5

Your government/corporate pension, combined with CPP, will take you through to 100.

We suggest that, unless your pension is ample, defined-benefit and inflation-proof, it's a good idea to plan to earn some income after 60 or 65.

Only a small percentage of working Canadians now in their 40s and 50s can expect to receive "gold-standard" pensions, the kind that pay a defined amount each month and that increase with inflation. Most of them have worked for extended periods for government or for a large company in an established industry.

Those of us who have to make do with the much more common "defined contribution" pension plans—or with RRSPs (Registered Retirement Savings Plans)—as our tax-advantaged retirement savings vehicles can derive some comfort from the fact that fewer and fewer employers are offering the gold-standard plans any more. The reason is cost; it's just too expensive. Think about it: how many pension plans not backed by the taxing power of the government of Canada are likely to be able to afford to pay indexed, defined benefits to 55-year-old retirees who may well be around to receive pension benefits for a period longer than their entire working lives?

It won't have escaped you that CPP (Canada Pension Plan) contributions are going up—way up. As recently as 1993, employer plus employee contributions totalled 5 per cent of wages; in 2003 and subsequent years, contributions will be

9.9 per cent, or almost double. These increases reflect the declining dependency ratio, that is, the number of workers available to pay the pension benefit for each retiree. Many actuaries and economists predict that the rates will have to go even higher to keep the pay-as-you-go system solvent. Demographers predict that there will be fewer than two working stiffs for every retired person in Canada by 2026. And since very nearly all the donors and the recipients (except for future immigrants) are already working their way through the system, the only way to improve the ratio is to reduce the number of retirees by working longer. (There is very little support for reducing the number by increasing mortality.)

Canadians are living in a low-inflation environment, and the well-organized, vocal and numerous ranks of CARP (Canadian Association of Retired Persons; now known as Canada's Association for the Fifty-Plus) will make it very uncomfortable for any future government to adopt inflationary policies. So it is really hard to imagine a return to the inflation levels of the 1970s. But, just for a moment, think back to Myth #3 above. Labour shortages can be very inflationary as employers bid up wages to get the workers they need. Also, if all the baby boomers retire and send the dependency ratio to new highs, those who are working may view inflation as the most expedient way to reduce the real amounts they have to pay to baby boomer retirees via their payroll and other taxes. Not a pretty picture for those without gold-standard pensions!

We think there's a potential deal here. It goes something like this: baby boomers—or at least the best educated and most highly experienced of them—will keep working to age 70 or even 75. The labour shortage will not be so severe as it otherwise would be, so inflationary pressures will be reduced. Also, the additional payroll taxes boomers pay will help fund the CPP benefits paid to those who are disabled or not in demand. In return for the boomers' stalwart assistance in lessening their tax burden, younger taxpayers may decide that inflating the boomers out of their pensions is not necessary after all.[5]

Myth #6

After age 65 you will probably be physically or mentally disabled, so you'll be unable to work, volunteer or participate actively in society.

> **The fact is, most boomers won't be "old" at 65, and many will be fit and healthy well past 75.**

Let's face it: unless they have the misfortune to be run over by a bus or crash into a mountain, most people will sooner or later become disabled in some way. That's the bad news. The good news is that evidence is mounting that increased longevity does not go hand-in-hand with longer periods of disability. In other words, just because you can expect to live longer than your parents and grandparents does not mean you should also expect more years of decline and dependency than they experienced.

Statistics Canada surveys consistently show that more and more seniors are living well into their 70s and 80s without substantial disabilities.[6] What appears to be true is that today's seniors are staying healthier longer. They owe this to improved health care, those many hours spent getting or staying fit and improved diet. There is also evidence for a link between maintaining activity levels and prolonged mental and physical well-being. So, not only are you likely to be able to exercise, work, volunteer and maintain an active social life after 65, but you can also expect that, if you do, your heath status will be affected positively.

So, does this mean that a traditional retirement is bad for you? Not exactly, though you can probably think of people who went from dynamic to declining soon after they stopped working. What it means is that many people are happier and healthier if they keep physically active and believe they are productive. What we feel is a good use of time—writing, tending flowers, going to a concert—may not be activities on your list, but you probably have such a list. Try writing it down. This is a good way to start planning for "retirement."

Myth #7

Filling up the time when you retire is a snap.

> **This may be true if all you want is to fill time. Most people want much more.**

If you are a normal A-type personality who works and commutes nine to 12 hours a day, full retirement will bring a windfall of time—between 2,000 and 3,000 hours per year. And, since you won't have a boss anymore, *you* get to decide what to do with it. The question is, after you've read the paper, walked the dog and put the breakfast dishes in the dishwasher, what will you do between 9 A.M. and 5 P.M.?

Many people have a mental list of projects we are "saving" for our retirements. Diane's favourite retirement project is listening to all the Haydn symphonies; the composer wrote 104 of them, and they are bright, cheerful pieces. Their total time is about equivalent to one week of work. Even when Diane adds in the re-upholstery of all the furniture the cats have shredded, there's a lot of time left to fill.

What about hobbies and volunteer work? The sad truth is that you are not likely to embark on entirely new activities the day after you retire. Research shows that retired people do the same things after retirement that they did before retirement—with the exception of their jobs. For those who do not have already established hobbies, volunteer roles or work commitments, the day is filled with housework, errands, yard work, watching television and visiting with friends and family. This is why women often adapt to traditional retirement better than their husbands do—they frequently have more varied non-work activities, which continue after they or their spouses retire.

As people approach traditional retirement age, most face for the first time the challenge of being accountable only to ourselves for the hours between 9 and 5. The self-employed have the most pre-retirement experience in this area, but even they have to meet the demands of clients—and, of course, the Canadian Customs and Revenue Agency. The question you need to ask yourself is: "Do I want to fill time, or do I want to find ways to make my time as productive and rewarding as possible?" We're betting that, if you're reading this book, you want to use time, not just fill it.

Most of us crave at least some structure in our lives. We like to know that someone is relying on us to finish a job or provide care or show up on time for an event. And recent research by AARP (formerly the American Association of Retired Persons) found that most boomers expect to continue working either for pay or as volunteers after they "retire"—many because they want the additional income, but equally as many because they derive feelings of satisfaction from working.[7]

Chapter 2

Demography Is Destiny

SHAKESPEARE, AS USUAL, had it right when he wrote in *As You Like It* of the seven ages of man. Man makes his entrance upon the stage as a "mewling and puking" infant, progresses through the "whining school-boy," the sighing lover and the soldier "full of strange oaths and bearded like the pard,/ Jealous in honour, sudden and quick in quarrel" (sounds a lot like today's aggressive bond trader) to the prosperous and rotund judge "full of wise saws." He declines into age and makes his exit from life's theatre "sans teeth."[1]

Although modern dentistry has preserved a lot more of the mature population's teeth in the past 50 years, the inevitable progress from infancy to age—and the number of years that progress takes—determine not only individuals' roles in society, but also many of the important characteristics of that society. Population dynamics are the slow-moving but irresistible determinant of a society's history.

If the birth rate rises, five years later the need for schooling facilities and teachers begins to rise. If medical breakthroughs extend life expectancy, more people will live longer after retirement and the demands on both public and private pension programs will gradually increase. While changes over short periods such as months or a year may scarcely be noticed, over time—like the hapless frog in the gradually heating cauldron—the people who have to provide schools or pensions find themselves in a lot of hot water.

If a large proportion of the population is concentrated in one age group—what demographers call a "cohort," such as the baby boomers—that group, as it passes through the seven stages, will have a large impact on the society. Shifts in both public and private consumption, in the political maturity of the electorate and in prevailing attitudes to everything from inflation to health care will result.

As people age, their patterns of consumption and savings change. In their early years, people move from disposable diapers to schoolbooks and home computers and save for that eagerly anticipated first car. Later, when courting, marrying and starting their own families, they buy refrigerators, sofas and child car seats and save for a down payment on a starter home. They then acquire mortgages and start building assets—first a home and then savings for the kids' university tuition and for their own retirements. Often, after the children graduate, more of the family budget is allocated to luxuries—travel, entertainment, a smarter car—though saving for retirement is also a high priority. Once employment income declines, previous levels of savings and the generosity of government pensions determine the levels of discretionary income—and, therefore, affect people's spending on goods and services ranging from quality wines to contributions to arts and culture. Now, the marketers of everything from durable goods to golf club memberships are working overtime to understand the impact of the aging of the boomers.

THE BOOMERS ONSTAGE

In fact, the impact of the boomers on Canadian society in the past half century has been significant and, to the ongoing chagrin of other age cohorts, will continue to be so for the next four decades at least. In the 1950s, they were a major cause of rapid growth in the housing industry. The one-bedroom apartment was no longer tolerable with two kids, so it was into bigger digs and, more often than not, a move to the suburbs. By the mid-1960s, the oldest of the boomers were teenagers and working part time. Individually they were not wealthy, but collectively they were numerous enough to create an unprecedented market for purveyors of fast food, blue jeans and inexpensive entertainment. During this time the pop music industry mushroomed, teenage movies became an identifiable product and the Pepsi generation was created.

By the late 1960s, the same generation was putting enormous strains on post-secondary institutions and entering the labour market in increasing numbers. Their rate of entry was faster than the economy could absorb, even though job creation was at record highs. What had been a labour shortage and a sellers' market for the children of the Great Depression was fast turning into a labour glut for the boomers. It produced a labour market in which employers seemed to hold all the good cards.

By the 1980s, large numbers of boomers were starting their own families and looking for suburban accommodation just like Mom and Dad's. Since their parents had no intention of moving out of their houses, the market for housing in most major urban areas in Canada began to heat up and stayed hot for a long time. (This is probably the source of the myth that real estate is always a good investment as well as a place to hang your hat.) Urban sprawl sprawled on, creating a host of challenges for beleaguered city planners, including urban traffic jams and many mismatches between the locations of students and schools.

By the 1990s, large numbers of the boomers were passing 40. Suddenly the generation that had cried "Never trust anybody over 30!" was middle-aged itself! Yesterday's flower children became obsessed with interest rates, the stock market and mutual fund returns. They wondered how they would pay for educating their kids and if they would be able to save enough for their retirements. They created a big market for RESPS and RRSPS and, as they inherited wealth from grandparents and parents, they formed a tempting market for those with skills in advising how wealth can and should be managed.

At the start of the 21st century, this same large group of boomers is again changing its tastes and consumption patterns. For many, the nest is empty and downsizing is an attractive option. There is no pressing need to replace consumer durables such as the fridge and stove—though boomers might splurge on a gourmet kitchen and cooking classes. They are more interested in travel opportunities and leisure activities than in new furniture. Significantly for our political leaders, many boomers have eschewed the carefree attitude towards inflation that characterized their 20s and are now demanding price stability as they approach that period of their lives when, more often than not, they will be living on fixed incomes. In both their personal lives and in public life, this means: pay down debt now, get expenditures under control and be prepared to make choices because you can't have everything. Sound familiar?

THE BASIC RULES OF DEMOGRAPHY

While marketers labour to understand the import of demographics for their sales projections, the rest of us also need to think about the population trends that are influencing major societal changes now—and that will continue to do so for the rest of our lives. As voters, we also have some decisions to make about how we want to see our society develop over the next 50 years.

Three factors contribute to the population dynamic: birth, death and immigration. Put simply, the only way you can have a 30-year-old in ten years is to have a 20-year-old alive today. Without immigration, there is no way there can be more 30-year-olds in ten years than there are 20-year-olds now. Indeed, given that there is some chance of death over the next ten years for anyone who is 20 today and there is the possibility that some will emigrate, it is almost certain that the number of 30-year-olds in ten years will be less than the number of 20-year-olds today. If you want more 30-year-olds, immigration is the *only* answer.

Significant and rapid shifts in the population don't normally happen. They build cumulatively over time and become clearly visible only after a decade or so. Yes, we can note a sudden shift in the birth rate or the death rate, but it takes several years of *sustained* change to make a noticeable impact on the structure of the population as a whole.

True, there have been natural catastrophes such as the Black Plague of the Middle Ages, when 25 per cent of Europe's population died in less than a decade. There have also been man-made catastrophes, such as the First World War, when about 10 per cent of France's male population died in five years. These horrific events resulted in a sudden and significant change in the structure of the population. However, events like this are rare. Population dynamics almost always evolve slowly, playing a profound role in determining history by affecting daily life economically, socially and politically.

Let's take a quick look at the three prime determinants of population dynamics.

Birth

The birth rate is the number of live births in a nation per 1,000 people per year. Canada's birth rate has been anything but stable over the past 100 years (see Figure 2). From 1911 to 1916, the birth rate was over 30 per 1,000. Then, beginning during the last years of the First World War and continuing through the Great Depression of the 1930s, when incomes fell precipitously and there was a great deal of economic uncertainty, the rate fell markedly to about 21 per 1,000. In the post-war period, with a

Figure 2: **ANNUAL NUMBER OF LIVE BIRTHS, CANADA, 1911–2000**
source: Urban Futures Institute

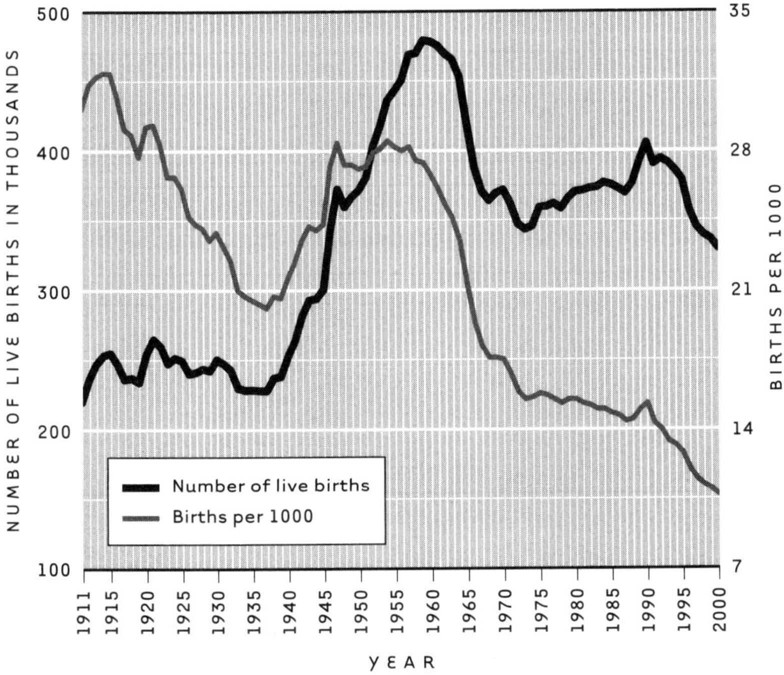

return to prosperity, birth rates rebounded to about 28 per 1,000—much closer to the rates that characterized the first years of the 20th century—and remained high until the early 1960s. The so-called baby boom was really just a return to the good old days!

In the 1960s, a number of widespread societal changes occurred simultaneously: reliable forms of birth control, increased participation by women in the labour force and the introduction of state-supported pensions all contributed to a decline in the birth rate. Since then, the rate has experienced a consistent and prolonged downward trend; today, the birth rate is a little over 10 per 1,000.

For a confirmation of these trends, let's look at another measure: the fertility rate. The average number of children born to a Canadian woman during her child-bearing years, which stood at 3.5 in 1921 and peaked at over 3.9 in the late 1950s, is now less than 1.5 (see Figure 3). This is well below the replacement rate, the rate at which the population remains stable in total numbers.

It's important to remember as well that changes in birth rates affect not only the absolute numbers of children born in any

Figure 3: **TOTAL FERTILITY RATE, CANADA, 1921–2000**
(Average number of children born per woman during her lifetime)
source: Urban Futures Institute

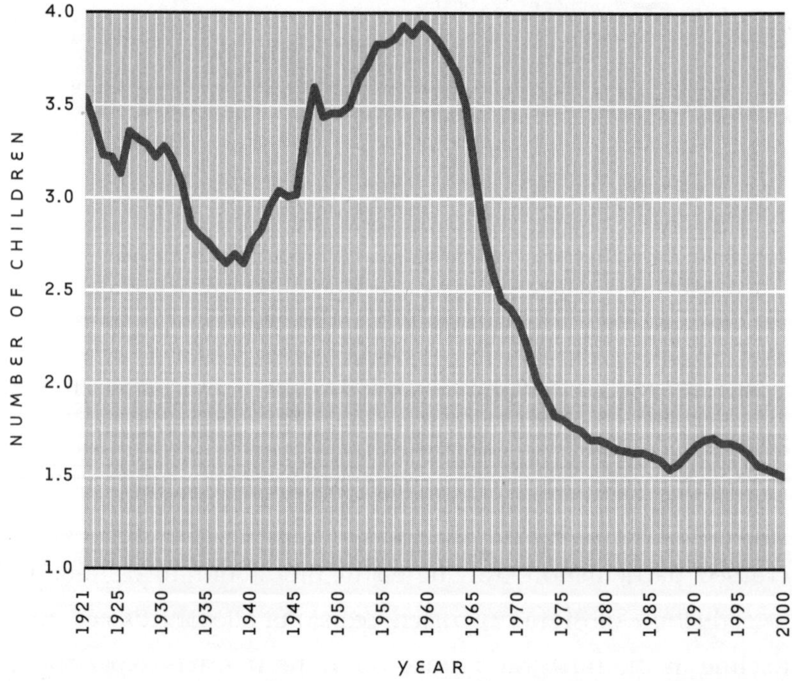

year, but also the resulting percentage of the total population occupied by each distinct cohort. For example, the Depression babies have always been a smaller proportion of the total population than have other age groups at a similar stage in their lives.

Likewise, the children born between 1948 and 1964, the boomers, are a disproportionately large percentage of the population and will continue to be so through the first several decades of the 21st century. In the current Canadian "population tree" (see again Figure 1 on page 26), the boomers are clearly identifiable as the bulge. Several other First World countries have similar population trees: Australia, New Zealand and the United States are like Canada in this respect. Many Third World countries, such as the Philippines, lack the bulge, so their trees have a different shape, with a wide base of young people and a narrow peak or summit of the elderly. For a graphic representation of this demographic reality, see Figure 4, which superimposes the population tree of the Philippines on that of Canada.

Look carefully at Figure 1. Notice that, after the boomers, the numbers in each ten-year age cohort are increasingly smaller. There is no marked "echo-boom," as some have called the over-hyped phenomenon of the boomers themselves having children—or, if there was one, it was very weak and sputtered out about six to ten years ago. The long-term trend is clear: smaller families and fewer children. Women are waiting till later in life to have their children and are having fewer of them. Fewer children today mean—barring immigration—fewer workers in future years. And fewer workers means not enough taxpayers to support social programs, including state pensions and health care.

Figure 4: **PERCENTAGE DISTRIBUTION OF POPULATION BY AGE AND SEX, CANADA AND THE PHILIPPINES, 2000**

source: Urban Futures Institute

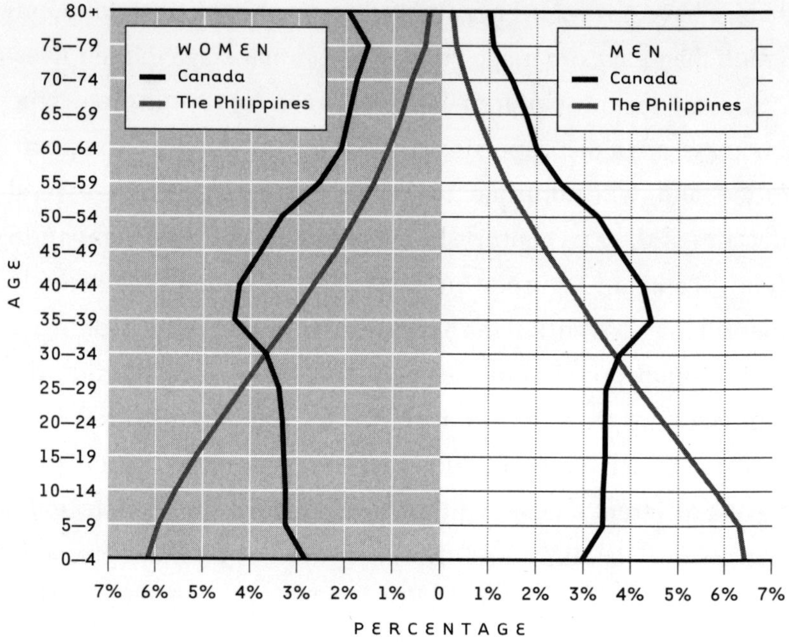

Some jurisdictions have tried to counter these trends by rewarding people who have larger families. Quebec, facing a lower birth rate than the rest of Canada, in 1998 introduced payments of $500 for each of the first and second child and $3,000 for the third and subsequent children (as eight quarterly payments of $375). The fertility gap between Quebec and the rest of Canada closed but at an estimated cost of $15,000 for each "extra" child.[2] The program was discontinued in 1997.

Clearly, if Canadian women don't want to have more children, nothing a democratic state can do—short of bankrupting the treasury—is going to change their minds. And, even if we abandon democracy and legislate family size (as they've tried in the People's Republic of China, with its own peculiar ramifications), the return on investment is about 30 years away. What to do?

Death

While we have yet to devise a method for keeping the grim reaper permanently at bay, at least in North America we have succeeded brilliantly in prolonging the period until his inevitable call. Among those who were born in Canada in 1921, life expectancy was 59 years for men and 61 years for women. For children born today, those same figures are 75.6 years for a male and 81.4 years for a female. That's a 29 per cent increase for the guys and a 33 per cent increase for the girls (see Figure 5).

It gets better for those who've made it to middle age. The typical Canadian aged 38 can probably expect to live to 80—almost a full decade more than a person of that age back in 1921. One of every eight males and one of every four females who are under of the age of 50 today will celebrate their 90th birthday. That compares with one in 20 at the start of the 20th century.

Moreover, all these numbers are probably conservative estimates. By the time the 38-year-old reaches age 65, he or she will not face the same probability of dying as does today's 65-year-old because there will be the added benefit for longevity of three more decades of medical research. Put another way, the youngest of the baby boomers, who will be retiring around 2025, can expect to live long enough to eventually be a problem not

Figure 5: **INCREASE IN LIFE EXPECTANCY IN YEARS, CANADA, BETWEEN 1921 AND 1996**

source: Urban Futures Institute

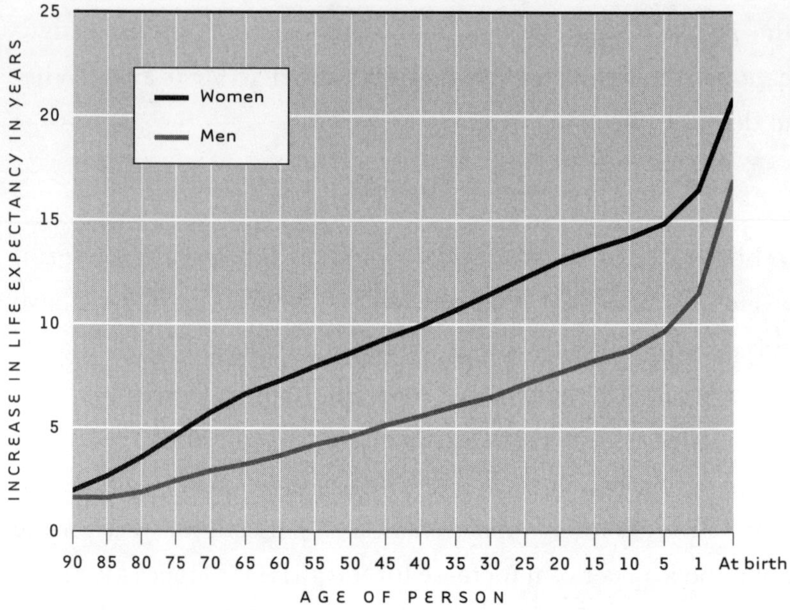

just for their children but also for their grandchildren, and probably for their great-grandchildren.

Why the big increase in life expectancy? First, medical research has successfully tackled the big killers of the first half of the 20th century: tuberculosis, influenza, pneumonia, diphtheria, appendicitis, measles, polio, rheumatic and typhoid fever, syphilis and others. The big killers are now accidents, violence, cancer and heart disease. Second, although accidents—particularly on the road—are major killers, industrial accidents have sharply declined in the past 50 years as safety practices and equipment have improved.

What this means is that there will be more old folks, not just because the baby boomers are fast approaching senior status, but also because those who are older than the boomers are still around and are likely to be so for some considerable time. This in turn means more people putting pressure on the health care system and more people collecting pensions. The water is getting very hot indeed if your job involves assuring the ability of public pensions and health care to keep pace.

Immigration

If passing laws to increase either birth or death rates seems a little too draconian for modern democratic sensibilities, then we can be very grateful that a lot of people who do not now live in Canada want to become Canadians. Immigration is the only major component of population dynamics over which the nation has some control. How many immigrants arrive each year can, over time, have a significant impact on both the size and structure of our population.

Consider first just the numbers. Without immigration, and given Canada's current birth rate, the population of Canada would slowly decline from the current 30 million to 28 million by 2045 and then decline sharply thereafter. This scenario is probably only really appealing to extreme environmentalists, who sometimes seem to prefer trees and bears to people. It is nothing short of horrifying to an economist or a business person hooked on the "virtuous circle" of economic growth.

The average intake of immigrants into Canada from 1986 to 1996 was 210,000, or about 0.7 per cent of Canada's population in 1996. If that intake were to be maintained—in terms of absolute annual net immigrations—until 2045, the population would rise to 40 million and stabilize shortly thereafter at about 42 million. Of course, freezing immigration at 210,000 per year means a declining *rate* of immigration; it eventually reaches 0.52 per cent in 2045. Just the same, we would have 12 million more people than without immigration. Moreover, if the *rate* were raised to 1 per cent (about 310,000 immigrants this year) and held constant at that level until 2045, the total population would be 51 million, implying some 500,000 immigrants in that year. That is 23 million more than if Canada had no immigration at all and about 8 million more than if it held the flow to 210,000 per year. These are not trivial differences; by any measure, the decisions Canadians make now about immigration will have a profound impact on the country their grandchildren will govern in their turn. The economists among them will be particularly pleased if any errors in immigration policy are on the side of more rather than less.

Now consider the impact that immigration has upon the structure of the population. The age profile of immigrants in recent years is distinctly younger than the Canadian population as a whole. For example, in 1996, two thirds of the immigrants were younger than 35, whereas half of the Canadian population as a whole was under 35. This trend tends to slow the aging of the Canadian population as a whole.

Consider this: if Canada stopped immigration today, by the year 2045 people 65 and older would comprise about 27 per cent of the population, compared to 12 per cent today. If it kept the flow at 210,000, and also assuming that the age profile of the immigrant population remains constant, those over 65 in 2045 would only constitute 23 per cent of the population, or 4 per cent less than with no immigration. Raise the rate to 1 per cent per year and hold it until 2045, and the impact is really dramatic. In 2045, the proporation of those over 65 falls to 21 per cent of the total population.

All of this can be translated into something called the dependency ratio, which compares the number of people 65 or older (assumed to be retired) plus the number of dependent children with the number of people of working age (those aged 15–64). The current ratio is 117 dependants to 1,000 working persons. Without immigration, by the year 2021 the dependency ratio will rise to 452 per 1,000, an increase of 286 per cent. With immigration held at 210,000, it will rise to 378 per 1,000, and with a 1 per cent annual immigration rate it will rise to 340, an increase of 190 per cent—still a staggering increase, but a lot less staggering than if there is no immigration.

Why all this concern about the dependency ratio? Well, it's the folks who work for a living who will provide most of the tax dollars needed to fund the social support systems such as health care and pensions. The more retired people that each one of these workers must support with his or her taxes, the greater the burden on each worker. The unpalatable options faced by the beleaguered worker are: less money spent on other government services, such as public education, or, if they don't want reduced services, higher taxes for working people. As many thoughtful pundits have observed, this is a recipe for intergenerational conflict. Put bluntly, the lower the dependency ratio, the less likely a taxpayer revolt. Remember Myth #5 about retirement income in Chapter 1 (page 32)—this is why it's a myth.

As David Baxter, Jim Smerdon and Andrew Ramlo of the Urban Futures Institute put it:

> Not only is immigration good for Canada's demography, it is good for Canada's economy: it increases the economic welfare of resident Canadians, creates employment, and makes Canada more economically competitive. Immigration—like education—is about investing in our future.[3]

BUT WHAT DOES THIS MEAN TO ME?

When the three factors discussed in this chapter—a highly variable and then, more recently, a steeply declining birth rate; increasing life expectancy, and a slowly declining *rate* of immigration—are combined, the future population profile of Canada carries some very sobering messages. Most particularly, these messages are relevant to the baby boomers and to succeeding generations.

First, if you are a boomer you can expect to live up to 25—or even 35—years after the age of 65 and possibly longer. Your retirement, if you quit work at age 65, may be of about the same duration as your working life. If you retire at 55, it could be much longer.

Second, the boomer bulge in the population structure is soon going to move from productive employment into the age of what we normally call retirement. The boomers will define retirement in their own fashion, just as they have defined many social constructs throughout their lives, but the fact remains they will put new demands on the economy and on society as a whole. They will increase demands on health care, especially after 2010, when the bulk of them start to creep into their 60s. They will, however, cling to their independence with the same fervour with which they once advocated world peace. Among other things, they will extend the frontier for the age at which people normally stop driving, providing unprecedented challenges for other drivers and the constabulary.

It is true that, some day, even the boomers will start dying in appreciable numbers, thereby lessening the strain upon the economy and society. Until then, however, the boomers will bring about a period of difficult adjustment both for each boomer individually and for society as a whole. On the other hand, the vast numbers of well-educated people with substantial amounts of free time could prove to be an unprecedented boon for our society.

Chapter 3

A Woman's Work Is Never Done

ONE OF THE GREAT "good news" stories of recent decades has been a large reduction in the percentage of Canadian seniors who live in poverty. According to Statistics Canada, fewer than 20 per cent of seniors now live in low-income situations, a statistic that improved dramatically between 1980, when 34 per cent had low incomes, and 1997, when the figure fell to 19 per cent.[1] There is some bad news, however. Unattached women (single, widowed or divorced) are greatly overrepresented in the low-income group; in 1997, almost half (49 per cent) of unattached senior women lived in low-income situations.

A few income numbers tell the story best. In 1981, the income of the average Canadian senior was $17,275 in 1997 dollars. In 1997, this average had risen to $20,451—about 75 per cent of the average income for Canadians aged 15 to 64. Most of this increased income to seniors came from CPP (or QPP in Quebec) pensions, employment pensions and RRSPs. The average breaks down, however, into a wide disparity by gender: total income for senior men in 1997 averaged $26,150, whereas for senior women it was only $16,070. Put another way, senior women enjoy only 61 per cent of the income received by senior men. Women also rely much more than men on Old Age Security, a government transfer program intended to reduce poverty among seniors. They typically receive much less of their income from retirement pensions—a reflection of their lower participation in full-time paid employment in their younger years.

This book, for the most part, discusses planning and preparation for retirement from the point of view of people who have worked for most of their adult lives. These are people who reach 60 or 65 having amassed CPP and pension entitlements or RRSP assets and a long résumé of formal experience in the paid workforce. They are in the enviable position of having both a reduced need for income from work and valuable experience that can produce income if needed. But there is also a large group, predominantly female, who are not in this advantageous position.

First, some background. As with other phases of life, the individual's expectations and experience of retirement are strongly influenced by his or her gender. Just as women's career paths—radically altered though they have been in the past 50 years—still differ significantly from men's, so do women's psychological and financial preparations for retirement. And, as with so many other dispatches from the front in women's drive to greater equality and independence, there is both good and bad news.

LONGER RETIREMENTS AND FEWER SAVINGS

The most worrying news is that women, as a group, are financially less well prepared than men are for retirement. They tend to have shorter working careers, usually because of time taken out of the workforce to fulfill family responsibilities. In general they earn lower wages and have a lower labour force participation rate (the percentage of a population—in this case, Canadian women—who are employed in the paid workforce).

These factors, combined with the female population's longer life expectancy, mean that women—again, as a group—acquire fewer pension assets, lower CPP entitlements and fewer RRSP assets than men do. Since they can expect to live in retirement for a longer period of time than men will, a mismatch exists between the resources available to support a comfortable retirement and the period of time women, on average, should expect to live after normal retirement age.[2]

Women, on average, also retire from paid employment at a younger age than men do, lengthening their retirement years effectively at both ends, compared with men's retirement. Why? Some leave their employment because the cost of doing so is not all that great—given that the average annual earnings from employment for women are only about 62 per cent of the earnings enjoyed by men. Some leave the workplace because the mortgage is paid off, the children have graduated from university and the family's need for a second income is reduced. Still others leave to take up yet more family responsibilities:

to provide home care for aging parents or daycare for their grandchildren.

But other women find themselves tied to their jobs out of sheer economic necessity for years after they would prefer to retire. A shorter number of working years before age 55—due to time taken to raise children or to support a husband's career as a "corporate spouse"—can translate into reduced benefits from an employer's pension plan or from CPP and more years of the daily grind after 55. And, after all, if women's wages are still significantly less than men's, even a lifetime of work and responsible money management can result in insufficient income from savings and pensions to allow a 60-year-old secretary to retire comfortably. This is especially likely to be true if she is single, widowed or divorced. In fact, almost 50 per cent of senior women who live alone do so in low-income circumstances (as defined by Statistics Canada).[3]

As long as women are married or living with other family members, individual income and assets matter less to their standard of living than do the family's collective financial resources. The catch is that, due to women's longer life expectancy and the long-established tradition of women marrying men who are somewhat older than themselves, the majority of senior women can expect to live alone for a number of years (see Table 1). In 1996, 46 per cent of all Canadian women 65 and over were widowed and a further 12 per cent were divorced or single. And senior women who do not live with spouses, partners or other family members live in more straitened circumstances than do most other Canadian seniors.

Table 1

Family Status of Women by Age, Canada, 1996

	Living with a spouse or partner	Living alone or with non-relatives
15–64	59.7%	13.6%
65–74	54.9%	31.5%
75–84	30.9%	50.9%
85+	11.0%	59.8%

Source: Statistics Canada, *A Portrait of Seniors in Canada,* 3rd ed., 89-519-XPE, page 39.

On the other hand, sombre though the statistics are, the trends are going in the right direction. Each cohort of Canadian women born since the 1930s has attained increased levels of education and labour force participation over earlier cohorts. Low-income rates among single senior women declined from 72 per cent in 1980 to 49 per cent in 1997 and will continue to decline as more and more women retire from longer careers in better-paying jobs. Let's look at some of the trends underlying these numbers.

EMPLOYMENT TRENDS FOR WOMEN AND MEN

Increasing workforce participation by women aged 25 to 64 was one of the most important sociological and economic trends of the last quarter of the 20th century. Another, less visible, trend has been the decline in workforce participation by men, particularly those aged 55 to 64. Table 2 summarizes the trends in percentage of the population—by both gender and age group—employed for 1976 through 2000.

Table 2

Percentage of Women and Men Employed, by Age, Canada, 1976–2000

	Women Aged			Men Aged		
	25–44	45–54	55–64	25–44	45–54	55–64
1976	49.9	45.6	30.4	90.9	88.9	72.8
1986	66.2	55.8	30.3	86.2	85.9	62.6
1996	70.9	66.2	33.6	82.9	82.4	53.7
2000	75.2	71.5	39.3	86.5	84.4	57.7
% Increase/Decrease, 1976 to 2000						
	50.7	56.8	29.3	−4.8	−5.1	−20.7

Source: Statistics Canada, *Women in Canada: Work Chapter Updates,* August 2001, 89FO133XIE.

Here we see two major trends interacting: for women from 25 to 54, the increase in the percentage employed (that is, their labour force participation rate) was stunning—over 50 per cent. Men in the same age cohorts experienced decreases in the percentage employed of about 5 per cent. For older men aged 55 to 64, we see clearly in the above numbers the trend towards earlier retirement, in which there was a sharp decline in the percentage employed, from 73 per cent in 1976 to 54 per cent in 1996. For women in the same age group, the percentage employed increased by 29 per cent—a large increase, but less than for their younger counterparts, because women were also affected by the trend to earlier retirement.

Interestingly, the statistics for older men show a rebound to about 58 per cent employed in 2000. It may be early to say this constitutes a major shift, but it would seem to be supported by anecdotal evidence that the trend among men to earlier and earlier retirement has been halted if not reversed. It could be explained by a decrease in the use by employers of early retirement to downsize their workforces, or it could reflect an improvement in the attractiveness of the employment opportunities available to older men. Or it could be symptomatic of a widening recognition that early retirement isn't everything it's cracked up to be.

Of course, the days when any First World country could contemplate running an economy without the widespread participation of women in the paid workforce are long gone. Overall, women accounted for 46 per cent of the employed workforce in 2000, up from 37 per cent in 1976. And 56 per cent of women aged 15 to 64 were employed in 2000, up one third from the 42 per cent who were employed in 1976. The impact was even more pronounced for well-educated women. For women with university degrees, the percentage employed in 2000 was 76 per cent—not a lot less than the 80 per cent employment rate for men with university degrees.

A closer examination of the numbers reveals that increases in the employment rate for women during this period were especially dramatic for women with children. Though still less likely to be employed than women without children, 70 per cent of all women with children under the age of 16 were employed in 2000. Also significantly, in the late 1970s, single mothers were more likely to be employed than were those in two-parent households. By 2000, there was a major shift: 63 per cent of single mothers were employed, whereas 71 per cent of mothers with partners were in the paid workforce. These trends constitute a social revolution.

Some important differences exist between men and women in their working lives, however. Women continue to make up the large majority—70 per cent—of those employed part time (less than 30 hours per week). In 2000, almost two million Canadian women had part-time jobs. Most of these women either didn't want a full-time job or found that working part time helped them to meet their child care or other responsibilities. Only 24 per cent of those surveyed would have preferred full-time employment.

Further, self-employment has grown dramatically among women. In 2000, almost one million Canadian women were self-employed, though they were still less likely than men to be self-employed: women accounted for 35 per cent of the self-employed in 2000, up more than a third from 26 per cent in 1976.

What these numbers reveal is that, over the past 30 years, women, including mothers of young children, have entered the workforce in ever-increasing numbers. To the extent that conventional full-time employment has not meshed readily with their family responsibilities, they have turned to part-time work and self-employment to attain the desired flexibility in or control over their schedules. So, while today's working women are amassing greater pension assets than their mothers and grandmothers ever imagined, the choices many make to better accommodate their roles as mothers, daughters and wives mean that their pensions will still fall short of those that their husbands and brothers can reasonably anticipate receiving when they retire.

A PREDOMINANTLY FEMALE SENIOR POPULATION

In 1998, women constituted 57 per cent of Canadians aged 65 and over. Among Canadians 55 and older, women outnumbered men (see Table 3). In short, women on average simply outlast men on average. In 1996, a woman aged 65 could expect to live another 20 years; her male counterpart had a remaining life expectancy of 16 years.

Table 3

Percentage of Women in Total Population, by Age Group, Canada, 1998

Age Group	Percentage Female
Under 55	50% or less
55–64	51%
65–74	54%
75–84	60%
85 and older	70%

Source: Statistics Canada, *A Portrait of Seniors in Canada,* 3rd ed., 89-519-XPE.

In 1996, 29 per cent of all seniors lived by themselves—a large increase over the 20 per cent who did so in 1970. And of course, because women outnumber men in the older age groups, senior women are far more likely than other Canadians to live alone. In 1996, 38 per cent of women aged 65 and over lived alone (compared with only 16 per cent of senior men). The pattern is even more pronounced among older groups: 58 per cent of women over 85 and 49 per cent of women aged 75 to 85 lived alone. Most of these women were widows.

MAINTAINING INDEPENDENCE FOR SENIORS

For most seniors, the foundation of independence is their ability to continue living in their own homes. And, in fact, the vast majority of Canadian seniors lives at home—in 1996, the percentage living in a private household, either with family or alone, was 93 per cent. Only 7 per cent lived in an institution, most in special care homes for the elderly and chronically ill. In part because of their greater longevity, women in the older age ranges are the most likely among seniors to live in an institution.

The ability of so many seniors to live independently reflects a major increase in the number of years Canadians can expect to live free of acute illness or serious disability. Most seniors living at home consider themselves to be in good health; in 1996–97, 78 per cent said their health was good, very good or excellent. The majority of the group, however, had been diagnosed with one or more chronic health conditions, such as arthritis or diabetes. Managing these conditions effectively is critical to maintaining good health and independence.

Supporting seniors' prized ability to live in their own homes are a wide array of formal and informal support services; in 1996, an amazing 84 per cent of all Canadians 65 and over received assistance with household work and other tasks of daily life, such as shopping, banking and bill-paying. Most of this help came from family and friends—though 10 per cent of seniors got support from a home care service.

HISTORY AND HEALTH CARE: MARGARET LABARGE

Margaret Labarge is a force for civilization. To sit down at dinner with her—as we did recently at a friend's house in Ottawa—is to embark on a guided tour of the major preoccupations of our society. As a historian, Margaret is steeped in medieval history, but there is nothing medieval in her approach to life or to the business of making Canada a better place to live. In her mid-80s, she seizes upon new ideas and incorporates them into her world view with the enthusiasm of a graduate student.

Margaret was born into a well-to-do New York family. She earned her undergraduate degree at Radcliffe and then went on to study medieval history at Oxford, where she met her Canadian husband, Raymond Labarge. Their studies were cut short when the Second World War brought them back to North America. They married in 1940, and Margaret embarked on the life of a civil servant's wife in Ottawa, raising four children while maintaining the social obligations expected of the spouse of a rising mandarin. She found time, however, to keep her oar in the academic world, lecturing part time at local colleges and universities. Then, in the early 1960s, she published the first of nine books on medieval history, both scholarly and popular. Probably her best-known book is

Women in Medieval Life, published in 1986, which earned her a Governor General's Award.

Yet for Margaret, the life of a scholar—with its necessary isolation—seemed incomplete and unbalanced. As her children became more independent, she pursued a developing interest in public-health issues, first by serving on the board of a Catholic hospital in Ottawa. "They wanted my husband, of course," she recounts, "but they had to take me." It was the beginning of a long career of volunteer commitment that took her into all the pressing policy issues facing publicly funded health care in the 1980s and 1990s. She served as a public representative of the board of the Canadian Nurses Association and on the Catholic Health Association of Ontario as a director and then as president. She became a lay expert on health care for the aging. She also volunteered her time as a governor of Carleton University.

Raymond Labarge's early death from a heart attack in 1972, at about the time Margaret's youngest child was ready to leave home, brought a sudden and extreme quiet to the hitherto lively Labarge family home. Faced with an unexpected and tragic discontinuity in her personal life, Margaret found the balance she had carefully cultivated between her solitary scholarly life and her volunteer involvements in the health care sector a boon. Financial security was no problem, so she was free to pursue both her vocation of scholarly research and her avocation in health care services and issues. So effective was she in her volunteer roles that, in 1982, Margaret Labarge received the Order of Canada. Of course, having achieved this recognition, she redoubled her efforts.

An area of increasing interest for Margaret as she grew older was the provision of health care and other social services to Canadians as they age. Fully aware of the implications of the greying of the population for publicly funded health care, she pointed to the pivotal role that volunteers will play in providing the many services that the coming bumper crop of seniors will need. These services include not only health care, narrowly defined, but also the simple support services that can allow frail seniors to continue living in their own homes—a happier, and cheaper, alternative to life in an institution. And it is clear who is going to be providing these services: women. As Margaret said, "The men won't do it!"

Her cheerful, practical recognition of the expectations society places upon women to be caregivers—whether to their own family members or to others—cast a sudden illumination on an issue that had recurred again and again in our research and reading. The burgeoning cost of health care for our growing senior population is beyond the state's ability to finance through increased taxes. This cost represents a large, unfunded liability that can sink provinces—and their debt ratings—if ways are not found to provide services more efficiently. And there are few more cost-effective resources available to the troubled system than the contributed time, knowledge and compassion of well-educated women who no longer work full time and whose children no longer claim the lion's share of their caregiving capacities.

Margaret can truly be said to have shouldered more than her share of our society's work of recalling and learning from our past, as well as building institutions that will serve us in the future. However, her influence in her personal relations is just as important. Her example is both inspiring and practical; she shows those around her daily how the wisdom of age can be channelled into work that is fulfilling and productive. After an evening with her, you say to yourself, "Oh, if only I can be that vital when I am 85!"

So, how to achieve and maintain this vitality? Good health and an indomitable spirit certainly help. But you can also learn some lessons about the mind–body connection.

- The ardent pursuit of an intellectual passion can be good for your health!
- A judicious balance between devotion to family, to society at large and to the life of the mind makes for a contented and productive life.
- Finally, engagement in the "big issues"—such as how to provide people with the health care they need and expect—may be challenging and frustrating at times, but it can also provide a mission in life long after the need to pay the mortgage and feed the family is past. And having a mission can also be very good for your health!

EMPLOYMENT AND VOLUNTEER ACTIVITIES AMONG SENIORS

Canadian seniors, women and men, for the most part enjoying good health, continue to be active. In 1998, only a fairly small percentage of seniors were still working in the conventional sense: 6 per cent of the total senior workforce had jobs, and many of these were self-employed and/or worked part time. A much higher percentage of seniors, however, regularly undertook work in a voluntary capacity: 23 per cent participated in formal volunteer activities by working with social service, educational and cultural organizations in their communities. This percentage is lower than the percentage of non-senior adults who volunteer, but the average amount of time contributed is higher for seniors.

Even more seniors—a stunning 58 per cent in 1997—participated in informal volunteer activities outside their homes, such as providing support to friends and family members: helping with child care, housework, shopping and financial tasks. Just as importantly, many provide emotional support and check on the well-being of friends and neighbours by visiting or telephoning. As in career choices, there are differences in the kinds of services provided by men and women. Generally, women help with housework, provide babysitting services, visit with other seniors and give care and support to the sick. Men are more likely to help with gardening, shopping and transportation and to perform handyman services. Thus, while many seniors receive assistance to maintain their independence, many also give assistance to others. It's a two-way street.

IMPROVING PROSPECTS FOR SENIOR WOMEN

The workforce participation data summarized above show that women who retire in the 21st century will probably do better than those who retired before 2000, simply because they have been employed for more years than previous generations of women had. And women's employment income, at least that of well-educated women, has increased compared with men's. Their retirement savings, whether in the form of employment pensions, CPP entitlements or RRSPs—all of which are linked to employment income and duration—will be greater. But it is still important to note that, especially for women who are not highly educated, a major gap will persist because they still work fewer years for lower wages than do men with comparable education levels. And, since so many women will continue to live a significant portion of their lives as widows and since the divorce rate remains high, the incidence of poverty among senior women will continue to be distressingly common.

What measures would significantly improve this situation? First, the retirement of mandatory retirement would help. Although many women voluntarily leave the labour force after 55—presumably because the income requirements of their families are declining—forced retirement at 65 or earlier really doesn't make sense and is arguably unfair to women. If a woman needs to continue to work to build up her retirement nest egg or CPP entitlement (perhaps because she took several years out of the labour force to raise children when she was younger), she should certainly be allowed to do so. After all, she will likely live longer than her male colleague, so her need for retirement assets is greater, not less, than his. Furthermore, organizations and companies increasingly and desperately need the skills many older women bring to the workplace, such as patience, willingness to listen to and help colleagues and sensitivity to the needs and concerns of the customer or client.

Second, early retirees and seniors who enjoy good health should be encouraged to provide volunteer or modestly paid services to others in their communities—even if they don't need to earn and save. Our society's need for the kinds of services that women whose own families are grown can provide—caring for children of working mothers, providing meals for homebound seniors and doing personal tasks for the frail elderly—will continue to grow rapidly as both the senior population and young mothers' participation in the workforce continue to grow. And mature, responsible and experienced women are a tremendously valuable resource that may be one of the last and best hopes we have to meet the burgeoning need for personal care and support created by our aging population.

How to mobilize this resource more effectively for the benefit of both the givers and receivers of care is worth some serious thought. Although it is good that many volunteer their time out of a desire to help their families, neighbours and communities, it is also appropriate that our society should recognize in a tangible way the value of these services. As is suggested in the next chapter, a tax receipt for the value of hours contributed—even if calculated at the minimum wage—would provide seniors who have a modest income with the chance to improve their financial position while they donate their time and skills to the service of others.

This overwhelming and growing need for able older people—especially women, since they are the majority—to participate more fully in the provision of care for society's dependent members is expected to drive a significant revolution in social policy over the next few decades. Now that provincial governments across the country are coming to grips—and none too soon—with the reality that the demand for health care is likely to grow exponentially over the next several decades, they are also recognizing that not every service can be provided by a unionized workforce in the direct or indirect employ of the province. There are several reasons for this, including the need for greater efficiency, but the most important is also the simplest: *We can't afford it!* At least, Canadians can't afford it if they also want to provide publicly financed education for their children and grandchildren, protection for their lives and their property, and good roads.

So, how will the slack be taken up? Politicians may be afraid to tell Canadians that the answer is: baby boom women. Whether their services are provided informally to friends and family members or formally through health care or educational organizations, whether they are paid or unpaid, they are essential to the well-being of our seniors and our children and to balanced provincial budgets. They will be delivered, not according to rigid job descriptions and work rules, but just as the providers want to deliver them, since the satisfaction of helping others on a personal level will be no small part of the reward the providers seek.

Linda Walker of Vancouver is a pleasant, outgoing woman who, in her mid-50s, wants to work only part time. Along with two other similarly situated friends, Linda has created entirely by word of mouth an informal network of local seniors who need practical help to maintain independence and stay in their own apartments. At the moment Linda has nine "clients"—not surprisingly, all women in their 70s and 80s—whom she visits regularly.

Linda and her friends do not provide health care; rather, they help their seniors with tasks they find too difficult to manage—everything from hanging a picture to doing personal shopping and errands. Linda recounts one case of a lady with arthritis who is unable to chop vegetables; Linda can do this for her when she visits twice a week, helping her maintain a healthy diet. And, with her background in hairdressing, Linda often does hair-styling or a manicure—a special feel-good treat for women who can no longer easily make the trip to a salon. "They all need different things," says Linda.

Linda and her friends fill an important and underserved niche. Home care workers in the health care sector cannot provide housekeeping services or run errands; given the pressures on the provincial health care budget, this is understandable. But without such assistance, many seniors would have to move into assisted living or long-term care facilities. Through the continuity provided by regular visits, Linda finds that she develops personal relationships with her seniors, who are comfortable calling on her if they need diplomatic help with a family problem.

An important service that Linda provides to her group of seniors is helping them deal with the bureaucratic aspects of the health care system. She will happily be a little aggressive about scheduling appointments or arranging home help after surgery, and she observes that those of her group who do best are those who maintain social contacts, perhaps through their bridge clubs or by helping out at the library.

It's easy to see that Linda and her friends provide a valuable service. It's also an arrangement that works well for them. When one of them is out of town on a family vacation the others can "cover," and Linda's part-time schedule leaves her time year-round for her personal passion, gardening.

WOMEN'S WORK

Diane's grandmother, a farmer's wife with a grade 8 education, was fond of encapsulating her considerable practical wisdom in rhyming couplets. One of her favourites was this observation on the lot of women in her not-so-long-ago world of heavy house and garden work: "Man may work from sun to sun/But woman's work is never done!" Grandma would then recount tales of her mother and grandmother sewing and darning socks late into the evening by the inadequate light of an oil lamp after already long days of cooking, cleaning and gardening.

The 21st century woman could be forgiven if she wonders if much has changed in any essential way. Now the exhausted career woman turns up for her "second shift" on the home front and the single mother struggles to pay the bills while desperately trying to be a full-time parent. The standard of living Canadian women enjoy may far outstrip that achieved by their foremothers, but many feel they have less and less of that priceless luxury: time for themselves, their interests and their friends. If truth be told, they may have about the same amount as their grandmothers did—and it was probably too little for them too.

Something they do enjoy that earlier generations did not was the prospect of many years of good health beyond those years traditionally dedicated to improving the life of their families. Their expectation is that the years after age 55 or 60 will be golden in the sense that there will be more time for personal or leisure pursuits long neglected for the sake of children or career. It's true that women made tremendous gains in longevity in the 20th century, far outstripping even the impressive gains made by men. When Diane's grandmother was born in 1890, her life expectancy was 54 years; when Diane was born in 1949, hers was about 71 years and it's now increased to 80. Grandma, of course, far outperformed the statistics—evidence, perhaps, that hard work isn't that bad for you. So, in the sense that this generation of women can expect, on average, a greater number of years of life than their spouses and our forebears, they have before them an unprecedented opportunity to make up for those years of too many tasks and too little sleep in their 30s and 40s.

Women need to give a lot of thought to how they want to use this opportunity. Fantasies of strolling sun-drenched beaches for 30 years are more attractive in the imagining than in the experience. Women whose working or family lives have been highly productive are more likely to look for ways to make a difference in the lives of others than for ways to dissipate unaccustomed leisure. The opportunities will be there, and women will be able to dictate the terms under which they take them up. This is a kind of freedom worth having!

A LONG LIFE OF LEARNING: SYLVIA OSTRY

Sylvia Ostry has always been a ball of fire. From her days as an undergraduate at the University of Manitoba, through graduate school at McGill and Cambridge, and then as a civil servant in ever more important roles in Ottawa, she was a vibrant and exciting person to work with and for. During the 1970s and 1980s, she and her husband, Bernard, were one of the star couples in the capital. Their razor-sharp minds and wide circle of friends gave them immense influence in the capital during the Trudeau and Mulroney years. Both were deputy ministers, both are members of the Order of Canada (Sylvia is a Companion) and both have left their mark on Canadian public policy.

Sylvia was the first woman deputy minister when she became chief statistician of Canada, then subsequently the deputy minister of consumer and corporate affairs, chairman of the Economic Council, undersecretary of trade and finally the prime minister's personal representative for the Economic Summit (referred to among insiders as "The

Sherpa"). In between the stints at the Economic Council and her work in External Affairs, she took leave from the Canadian government to head up the economics and statistics department of the Organization for Economic Cooperation and Development (OECD) in Paris. To call her an overachiever would be putting it mildly. As Sylvia says, "I never planned out a career. I just looked at opportunities for what they could teach me. The whole purpose of my career was to learn, and I was fortunate to have a range of opportunities where the learning was fascinating and valuable."

The government refused her request for an extension of her leave to the OECD, insisting she return to Ottawa—not to Finance, as she requested, but to International Trade. Looking back on this double disappointment, Sylvia considers it the best thing that ever happened to her career. "When I went to the OECD I really started to learn about macroeconomics, and when I returned to Ottawa as the undersecretary for International Trade I learned about a whole new and vastly complex subject area. I had wanted to be the deputy of Finance, but in retrospect I am so happy that I went to Trade since it literally opened the world to me. I was in at the beginning of the last great round of multilateral trade liberalization, and I met people from government, industry and academia that I might not otherwise have known. Moreover, I learned so much about what matters to nations in trade and how agreements are or are not reached."

When Sylvia's years in the public service drew to a close, she did not consider putting down her tools. She simply transferred herself and her formidable experience to the world of academic research, which, in any case, had always been her first love. In 1988, the Council on Foreign Relations in New York offered her a chair financed by the Volvo Motor Company, and she accepted it. This gave her time to write and to participate in a host of international forums, where her thoughts and insights were greatly appreciated. A year later, she moved to the University of Toronto's Centre for International Studies.

In both of these latter appointments, Sylvia joyfully cast off the administrative responsibilities that come with being a senior government official and threw herself into learning and research. Did she ever think of retiring? "Never!!! The opportunities and challenges for further learning just kept presenting themselves. There were always interesting problems to work on and people kept asking me to study this or that or participate in a host of forums."

Sylvia maintains that economists frequently make the mistake of assuming that work is a disutility—that it is something people only do because they need to earn a living—and that people will always prefer more leisure and less work. Sylvia herself certainly gives the lie to this generalization, as do many of the other vital and interesting people who were interviewed for this book. The secret is out! People who work when they no longer need to for financial reasons are neither irrational nor workaholics. They just take a lot of pleasure in learning, in exercising and improving their skills and in their interactions with colleagues and associates.

Sylvia believes that because she viewed every opportunity as a potential learning experience, the knowledge she gained along the way helped her to be successful and to draw great satisfaction from each of her successive positions. Most particularly, she feels that her international experience gives her a very valuable perspective. Grounded, as it is, in the real world of political and economic imperatives, it helps her see academic policy issues in a much different light than she would had she not had the experience.

Sylvia recalled Bernard Shaw's play, *Back to Methuselah,* in which the playwright explores the concept that humans are the only living creatures on earth for whom physical maturity and mental maturity do not coincide. She also believes that emotional and intellectual maturity arrive very late in life; she is, she says, still striving to attain them.

Sylvia's remarkable experiences affirm the long-term benefits of a career involving constant change and sometimes unanticipated turns. Your skills in learning and adapting come into their own!

- Seek challenges that play to your strengths—including the wisdom you have gained from all your previous experience. At the same time, slough off those tasks that provide you with neither enjoyment nor intellectual challenges.
- The experience you have gained in a varied career can enrich the learning experience in later life, bringing valuable perspective to both new and old subjects. In some

ways, it's like a masterpiece of oil painting. Each layer of paint—or experience—adds to the depth and luminosity of the image.

- The joy of learning can be lifelong.

Chapter 4

Why Traditional Retirement Should Retire

Ask any boomer worth his gourmet sea salt what intangibles he values and he'll probably tell you—in one way or another—that he likes choice, control and continuity—the three Cs.

In the realm of retirement planning, these values are reflected in our desire to have multiple options in terms of where we live, what we do and whether—or how much—we work. Further, we want to decide—with our spouses or partners and perhaps with our children, but most definitely *not* with Big Brother—when or if we should formally retire. And, most of us who enjoy at least some aspects of our working lives want to find some way to preserve those positive aspects—the intellectual stimulation, the human contact, and perhaps the compensation—even if we no longer want to go to the same office five days a week.

These values are totally negated both by the traditional "gold watch" retirement and by the euphemistic "early" retirement beloved of corporate downsizers, union organizers and human resources types. If your employer or the government tells you when to retire and you are expected to leave work one day and start stamp-collecting the next, you may just possibly feel tremendous liberation and relief. Perhaps not immediately, but within a short time thereafter, you are more likely to suffer the frustration and disorientation that human beings experience when deprived of choice, control and continuity. You will find yourself missing the daily mental stimulation you received while working and, unless you have planned carefully, finding a replacement for the benefits flowing from work will take time and thought.

The good news is that, over the next few years, labour market conditions will make it less and less attractive for employers to provide incentives for early retirement or to enforce a mandatory retirement age across the board. The simple reason is that replacing the skills and knowledge of retirees will be more and more difficult because replacement workers will not be as numerous. Moreover, this will not be a short-term phenomenon. Because the number of younger folks following on the boomer generation is smaller in absolute numbers, these market conditions will persist for decades at least. Compound the demographic factors with the potential for a mismatch between the skills available and the needs of employers, and the problem will become even more acute. The best that immigration can do, even if Canada recruits immigrants totalling 1 per cent of its total population each year, is to keep the number of replacement workers constant.

Under these conditions, companies wanting to grow will be

in a particularly difficult position. So the good employers will do what good companies always do in the face of a problem: they will get creative. Another C!

Examples of creative solutions already being tried across the country include such innovations as "phased retirement" and "consulting retirement." In phased retirement, the employee gradually retires over a number of years by reducing the number of days worked each week. In this process, he may also take on the role of mentoring younger employees who will eventually assume the retiree's responsibilities. In consulting retirement, the employee retires, perhaps even with the party and gifts, but comes back in the form of a consultant contracted to do only those professional tasks she is expertly qualified to do, while her administrative or management roles are taken up by others. For example, when David retired from the bank, he continued as a consulting economist speaking to bank clients and writing his weekly and quarterly economic letters. The consulting contract was for less than his normal salary, but his responsibilities and the time commitment were also reduced.

In both these scenarios, the retiree probably experiences a diminution in income, but pension benefits may offset this for some, and others may find the sacrifice well justified by the increased freedom to pursue other work or leisure interests.

In Japan, there is a well-established practice of moving older executives into less demanding roles—perhaps transferring them to a smaller company within the same group, or corporate family. Care is taken to ensure that the move is not characterized as a demotion, so there is no loss of "face."

Many individuals confronting unwelcome mandatory retirement have found a way around the system by becoming self-employed. In the opinion of some experts, the rise in self-employment in the last decade or more has been a form of disguised underemployment—or plain unemployment. But, more and more, self-employment is being recognized as a way to continue working past the age of 65 while gaining the ability to work on one's own schedule rather than an employer's.

What all these models share is a *flexible* approach to the institution of retirement. They recognize that increasing age does require adjustment, but that the best adjustments may be incremental in nature rather than "cold turkey." They also provide ways for the older worker to pass on valuable knowledge, maintain dignity and make a contribution commensurate with his or her individual capabilities.

Full of promise as some of these "flexible retirement" models may seem, the sad fact is that they are the exceptions. Too often, there are a multitude of barriers to their widespread adoption. This chapter deals with the institutional barriers you may face in devising a flexible retirement. These include:

- *Mandatory retirement:* Somebody else (your employer, your union or your government) decides when you must leave your current job.
- *Early retirement:* An employer offers to top up pension contributions so that the retiree suffers no loss of benefits because of the early retirement. This is typical in a downsizing action.

- *All-or-nothing retirement:* You must stop working entirely and abruptly rather than gradually phasing in retirement.
- *The pension fund trap:* Even if you can continue to work after 60 or 65, you may be denied the right to pay into the company pension plan. You can contribute to an RRSP to age 69, but you make *all* the contributions.
- *The CPP trap:* You can elect to start receiving CPP benefits at any time from age 60 on, but you have to be unemployed or at least 70 years old to qualify. The problem is, if you quit your job to qualify for CPP (which, remember, you have earned by making contributions) you may not be able to get it back, or get another job if you want to.
- *Retraining at your own expense:* If you need training to do another job after you are forcibly retired, the expense of that retraining is not deductible because of your age (if you are 65 or older).
- *Volunteering at your own expense:* If you have the resources to forgo earned income and you want to volunteer your time and expertise to a worthy cause, you receive no tax advantages for your volunteer work—as you would for a charitable contribution of cash or property.

Put another way, it almost appears that there is some sort of conspiracy to make sure that few if any individuals work past the age of 65. For some, this is not a problem—at least in the financial sense. But, for many, particularly those at the lower end of the income scale, being denied work or forced to take low-paying jobs because this is all that is available, regardless of their abilities, means mere subsistence rather than a dignified old age.

It is important, in planning for your later years, to understand that these rather mindless barriers exist and that they need to be torn down. All of these policies, both in the private and public sectors, can and should be changed. It's just a matter of focusing attention on these issues. What is required is effective organization by those who are or will be subject to these arbitrary barriers. We need to start pressuring employers and governments to change their policies and programs.

Fortunately, time and tides are on the side of change. The number of those coming face to face with these arbitrary constraints will rise as the boomers age. And, at the same time, so will the volume of their voices. Demographics and economics will eventually prevail, as they always do. But it would be both more practical and wiser if these barriers were taken down now so that society can begin to benefit from their removal as soon as possible.

These issues will pop up more frequently in public opinion polls in the next few years. Governments and business will take note—since boomers are important both as voters and as consumers—and retirement policy and age discrimination reform will become sexy topics of the day. At the end of this chapter, some specific suggestions appear that will help in the cause.

But first it is important to understand just how these barriers are constructed and how feeble are the rationales that underpin many retirement policies. The fine details don't appear here (look at some of the sources in the endnotes if you are a devoted policy wonk and just have to know), but each issue is outlined.

MANDATORY RETIREMENT

Mandatory retirement is the number one barrier. It is a polite term for employment discrimination—for being fired because of age. It became widespread during the 20th century. Its origins are both pragmatic and altruistic.

Pragmatism was a factor because mandatory retirement provided a means for organizations to rid themselves of deadwood. This was especially attractive in military organizations, which have seldom been a source of leading-edge ideas, especially any having to do with human resources. These organizations were concerned about senior officers who were well beyond their prime. Although this policy might throw out some good with the bad, it was felt, on the whole, that the costs were worth the benefit. That there was little empirical evidence to support this contention was beside the point. It had one great advantage: rules are rules, and mandatory retirement makes the question of leaving employment impersonal. No decision or emotion is involved: neither the employer nor the employee has any choice in the matter.

The altruism came from the belief of many social activists, particularly in the early part of the 20th century, that workers who had toiled, often at hard physical labour, for long years should be able to enjoy the final portion of their three-score-and-ten years free from work. Making retirement mandatory would prevent employers from exploiting the workers. Never mind that most workers would never reach retirement age; for those who did, no matter how short the period of leisure, the rule would be beneficial. The age of 65 was seen as a reasonable cut-off point. More years of leisure would never be accepted by the captains of industry, with or without pension plans for the rank and file. Of course, these social do-gooders seldom asked those who were the subject of this policy what they thought. It was just assumed that mandatory retirement was a good thing.

Whether altruistic or pragmatic, the underlying assumption was that of the traditional family: the husband working for one employer during his lifetime, and the wife working at home caring for children. All this has changed. Women have joined the paid labour force in great numbers. Many may have taken some years off for child rearing and therefore realize lower pension savings, but they also live, on average, seven years longer than men. So, in fact, they need greater pension assets than men do. Moreover, most workers are no longer engaged in heavy physical labour. The service sector employs the bulk of the labour force. Service jobs are more dependent on social and intellectual capital and the ability to continue to learn than upon physical prowess.

Mandatory retirement is a particular concern for two groups at opposite ends of the income scale. Many low-wage workers—especially women—do not amass adequate savings to support themselves and thus may face poverty if unable to work. (See Chapter 3 for statistics on poverty among Canadian seniors.) At the other end of the income scale are those with higher levels of education who often want to continue to work because of the intrinsically interesting nature of their jobs or professions.

Workers, both professional and blue collar, when faced with an employer's forced retirement policy, can try to find another comparable position. More likely than not, however, they will earn less for doing the same job they did before they reached 65. Further, they likely won't qualify for the same benefits that they enjoyed previously. If they face discrimination, they won't have the same protections that younger workers have under human rights legislation. They even enjoy lesser job security, in that they can be laid off or fired without cause.[1]

Mandatory retirement, which seemed such a good idea at one time, seems less wise now in light of significant changes in the conditions surrounding work and leisure. But perhaps it is not really surprising that mandatory retirement, as established in the workplace and institutionalized in law, is proving so difficult to change. Inertia, fear of change and a failure to appreciate the impact of demographic trends mean that most corporations, many unions and, not insignificantly, the Supreme Court of Canada have not yet come to grips with the inevitable.

The retention of mandatory retirement is usually justified by one or more of following economic or social arguments.

- Eliminating mandatory retirement would result in a massive disruption of the economy.
- Without mandatory retirement, companies would face substantial costs in the form of performance evaluations and individualized dismissals.

- Older workers are not as productive as young workers.
- Older workers, particularly in academia or in other environments where compensation increases with seniority, are very expensive.
- In unionized environments, some collective agreements say work ends at a certain age, and both labour and management have willingly agreed to the contract.
- Mandatory retirement ensures that employment opportunities are available for younger people.
- Mandatory retirement respects human dignity by avoiding the necessity of pointing out to some workers that they may no longer be able to make an adequate contribution to the endeavour.
- Age discrimination in employment isn't really discrimination; if it is, it is justifiable discrimination.

The argument that wiping out mandatory retirement would cause massive disruption in pension and heath care plans in the public and private sectors was a key argument used to support the retention of mandatory retirement when the Supreme Court of Canada ruled in favour of forced retirement in 1990.

In *McKinney versus University of Guelph,* the universities who supported mandatory retirement argued all of the standard arguments and added another.[2] Professorial salaries, almost without exception, were decided on seniority. That is, the older the professor and the longer his or her work record with a given institution, the higher the salary. Keeping people on after the age of 65 would, particularly in a period of restraint, severely handicap the university financially. The salary of a senior professor might equal as much as four salaries of junior faculty members who were just starting their academic careers. So mandatory retirement, it was argued, was important to allow the university to rejuvenate its faculty.

The decision of the court seemed to accept the employer's argument of skyrocketing costs without requiring any substantiation. The court also felt, in the case of tenured faculty, that the use of outside peer review would be particularly humiliating; it may have forgotten that granting tenure in the first place required such peer review and that most learned journals operate on the same principle of peer review.

An interesting point about this landmark case is that the universities involved made little attempt to find some compromise. Here's a solution that might have made everyone happy—without high legal fees. Retirement-age faculty members could claim the full amount of the pension they had earned, and at the same time, if the university wished to employ them, could continue to teach. They would receive a lesser salary but also would be relieved of the normal load of administrative duties carried by those of professorial rank (which few faculty enjoy anyway). They would still be able to make a contribution both to their students and their profession while freeing up salary dollars for the university. Of course, the university would need the option to allocate its budget elsewhere, and some would look for sinister motives if they did so. There might, for example, be a claim that older professors were denied continued employment because of their academic or political views rather than because of diminished mental faculties or declining student interest in their specialty. The resulting clamour of those who regularly defend the academic freedom of speech would serve as ample warning to institutions to avoid such shenanigans.

Of course, such a system relies on the professional comportment of the participants, and there could be abuse; no such scheme will be foolproof. It is, however, likely to result in better outcomes for many: good teachers will continue to inspire their students, the university will have greater budget flexibility and faculty members will be somewhat better off financially—and possibly much happier than if mandatory retirement had been enforced.

Universities seem particularly accident-prone in matters of retirement policy. In one case, upon reaching retirement age a professor was paid only half his salary because he was now collecting a pension. That continued until he sued and the university was required to pay him the portion of the salary he was denied. The university did, however, in the wake of the judgement, terminate his employment, much to the annoyance of his students, who thought him an excellent teacher.

In any case, no one knows in detail what the impact on government programs, employers or their pension programs would be in the event that mandatory retirement is retired.[3] No one knows how many employees would decide to stay on after 65. We are tempted to say simply: "Deal with it!"

The argument that the end of mandatory retirement would necessitate massive expenditures on performance evaluations and individualized dismissals fails upon close examination.

Implicit in this line of reasoning is an assumption that younger workers are not subject to performance evaluations—a clearly invalid assumption. An alternative assumption that, after a certain age, evaluations must be both more comprehensive and more complex than they are for younger workers is also inherently illogical. The situation is simply that there are costs to employing people of any age. Every employer must find ways to evaluate each employee's contribution to the common endeavour and to terminate those employees who are not pulling their weight—be they 25 or 65. Indeed, one suspects that mandatory retirement rules are perpetuated primarily for the benefit of human resources departments because they allow a strategy of delay rather than of facing up to difficult decisions, such as: "We don't have to terminate Frank, even though he hasn't picked up a new account in three years, because he's 58 and he'll be retiring soon anyway."

The idea that elderly workers are somehow less productive is not supported by the facts. There are, of course, exceptions. Professional athletes, ballet dancers, opera singers and other workers whose occupations rely upon certain physical capacities undoubtedly suffer deterioration in their capabilities over time. But to apply this universally to all occupations regardless of the nature of the activity and to further assume that it occurs in every line of endeavour at the same age is just nonsense. Does a barber or hairdresser become less efficient on the day he or she turns 65? Does the banker lose the ability to make credit judgements, the baker the ability to proof bread, the lawyer to understand and argue a case?

A raft of evidence both from the workplace and from various studies reported in the learned journals shows that the ability to perform mental tasks and to learn new tasks does not suddenly deteriorate with age. Nor does the evidence support the contention that disability or bodily deterioration generally occurs at the same age or at the same rate for all individuals.

The last four reasons given above to support mandatory retirement have more to do with societal values than with economics. They may sound good but, in fact, are equally indefensible. Union leaders, in particular, have been strong advocates of a fixed retirement age, originally for the altruistic reasons discussed at the beginning of this chapter and, more recently, as a means of opening up positions for new or younger workers—and not-so-incidentally augmenting their membership rolls. Chapter 1 demonstrated the wrong-headedness of the argument that mandatory retirement is necessary to free up spaces for younger workers. Possibly such an argument could be made in an age of surplus workers but certainly not in the coming decades, at least in Canada. Rather than experiencing a shortage of work, Canada will have a prolonged and chronic shortage of qualified workers.

Arguing, as some union leaders do, that since retirement age is often set down in collective agreements it is therefore defensible under the law of contracts is also specious. Workers, in effect, may have had little or no input into the details of a contract, even though they are held to its terms—and they may have widely divergent views about a provision that says they must cease work at age 60 or 65.

The argument that mandatory retirement protects human dignity is perhaps the most pernicious of all. In essence, it says that mandatory retirement protects the individual from the humiliation of being told that he or she is no longer able to carry out the responsibilities or tasks the job requires. Frank and factual worker evaluation is a fundamental of any effective human resources management program. To imply that once people reach a certain age they must be spared a realistic and unbiased appraisal is just nonsense; moreover, it is patronizing.

Arguing that age discrimination is not really discrimination because it is enshrined in a policy that is applied equally to everyone in a given firm does not remove the fact that such policies deny the individual employment. Age discrimination is not justified, humane or even practical. It deprives people of the opportunity to earn a living without regard to their knowledge, ability, financial resources or wishes. It hurts both society and the economy.

There simply is no valid justification for mandatory retirement. And the sooner employers and unions abandon it, either willingly or when forced to do so by law (as is already the case in Quebec and Manitoba), the better off we shall all be.

THE SIREN SONG OF EARLY RETIREMENT

Unlike mandatory retirement, which has an unpleasant sense of coercion, early retirement sounds great to many—employers and employees alike. The employer hears "reduced overhead"; the employee hears "School's out!" Many employees make early retirement the goal of their financial planning and savings program. But early retirement has become institutionalized in ways that do not produce good results either for the nation or for many individuals.

Two widely held beliefs underlie the rationale for early retirement. First, it is believed that some jobs are innately suited only to young people. Either they involve substantial risk or they so favour the strength and agility of youth that the effectiveness of persons working beyond a certain age or number of years is greatly reduced for all but a few of those involved in the activity. Police work and the armed forces are two such types of work; airline pilots are another.

The other principal rationales behind early retirement are based on the "lump of labour" fallacy, which was discussed earlier: there is only so much work to be done, and it needs to be shared by the population so that everyone has a chance to earn a living. Others consider early retirement a reward for having worked hard and saved diligently so that the retiree can enjoy an extended period of leisure.

For some, the opportunity to stop working—to try something different—is a great attraction, but that does not mean it is everyone's cup of tea. Work is not universally drudgery. As one economist working full time after normal retirement age said, "Economists make the mistake of assuming that work is always a disutility." In the real world outside the economics textbooks, work is stimulating and enjoyable for many. It offers an opportunity to meet and interact with other people, to pursue intellectual challenges and to make a contribution to society. Early retirement deprives such individuals of important emotional and social benefits as well as income. It may even lead to a rapid deterioration in mental and physical health as the retired person becomes bored with limited forms of stimulation and frustrated by a feeling of not contributing to society.

Promoting early retirement may in fact be imposing on all workers an ideal or objective that many, on reflection, find very unappealing. The more it is advocated, the wider its social acceptance, the more unwilling retirees believe they are acting in an anti-social fashion if they do not acquiesce to such a scheme at their workplace. Few outcomes are more illogical or undesirable in today's economy, for either the employee or the employer.

Consider early retirement from the point of view of a company's board and senior management. Early retirement is a strategy often used by companies that are attempting to downsize their labour force and is offered to employees as a one-time "get them while they're hot" benefit. This is a reflection of a serious lack of strategic thinking coupled with an obvious bias of age discrimination. The reasoning (if you can call it that) goes somewhat along these lines:

In order to reduce expenses, we need to reduce our labour force. The most expensive, in terms of benefits cost, and the least productive are the workers over, say, 55. (We are very wise and know age is a good proxy for productivity.) Why not offer all workers over 55 enhancements to the regular pension package as an inducement to leave voluntarily? We can determine the cost of such a program and therefore calculate with certainty the net cost to the company. And we'll get a triple benefit: we'll reduce the wage bill disproportionately, improve productivity and—not so incidentally—save the personnel department the task of sorting through the workforce and getting only the poorest performers to leave.

One factor this reasoning obviously ignores is that the senior workers are more likely to have the experience and familiarity with the operation that younger workers have yet to accumulate. Put in terms that a financial manager would use, the company's program of early retirement is implicitly putting a value of zero on the human capital and experience embodied in these senior workers. Were companies to assign a market value to this important asset in their cost-benefit analyses, a great number of early retirement programs would be set aside for a more effective form of human resource management.

And if many private-sector companies have unthinkingly shot themselves in the foot with early retirement programs, many government departments have managed practically to amputate their operations at the hip. The public service at the federal, provincial and often the municipal levels has put into place the same sort of regime for pensions that exist in the police, firefighting and armed services. That is, pensions are maximized under a formula that adds years of service to age; once this sum reaches an arbitrary maximum, 35 years' service and at least age 55, further years of work will not result in a more comfortable pension entitlement. You may certainly work until age 65. But, if you reach 35 years of service at, say, age 58, then your pension is maximized and working beyond this age results in no further increase in pension. If you go on working with your wage unchanged, you would, in effect, be working for a fraction of what you were earning prior to your 58th birthday. Why not retire and perhaps do something else—such as consulting to government? In short, the public service pension scheme encourages early retirement. This means the government is valuing the human capital provided by their older workers at zero.

We have to ask why such a pension scheme was made applicable to civil servants. These workers face no risks equivalent to those of police or the armed forces. Unlike pilots, they are not responsible for the lives of passengers. In fact, many work in analytical, research or policy-making positions where the returns on experience are great. What is the justification for such a scheme? In the debates of the House of Commons when the pension scheme was approved, it was just assumed that, if some (the armed forces) were offered this scheme, it was "only fair" that it be extended to other civil servants. Once instituted at the federal level, the argument was advanced that to "remain competitive" for personnel the other levels of government had to implement similar programs.

There was no impassioned debate; in government, such "housekeeping" matters normally receive scant attention from politicians, who are more focused on programs that affect the public. So, this distortion favouring early retirement in the public service entered into the system—and for many years has generated cadres of consultants on indexed pensions selling their services to governments—often to their former departments or agencies.

The folly of such a system is now evident. Within a very short period of time, as myriad boomer bureaucrats arrive at the magic level of pension maximization, they will be inclined to take the money and run, leaving governments bereft of their experience. Put yourself in their shoes. Would you continue to work for the same salary when you could get 70 per cent of it with no effort whatsoever? Especially when you could get another job that, as long as it paid more than 30 per cent of your previous salary as a civil servant, would put you ahead of the game?

Exactly!

UNEXPECTED OPPORTUNITY: THOMAS McCABE

Tom McCabe is a people person. He just likes talking with people, and that talent served him well as he worked his way up through the organization of one of Canada's major banks during a career of 34 years. In 1995, after seven years in charge of the bank's operations in Alberta, when forced to choose between moving yet again and taking care of his terminally ill mother, he found himself unexpectedly retired at the age of 55.

To say he wasn't ready for this step is putting it mildly. Despite his "golden handshake," he felt angry and betrayed—but not for long. As a result of his volunteer work, he had lots of good contacts in Calgary. He soon had a contract to privatize Alberta Tourism; that job lasted for 18 months. He then began work as a management consultant with a major firm in Calgary, one of whose clients was Theatre

Calgary, a not-for-profit company that had been suffering severe financial problems. As it happened, Tom had been chairman of the theatre's board of directors in his banking days and had been instrumental in getting the consulting contract placed long before he joined the firm.

It was clear that Theatre Calgary needed new professional direction. After Tom had made his consultant's report, the theatre group asked him to describe the characteristics of the new CEO. When he was finished they replied, "You mean somebody just like you." He replied in the affirmative, and within a few weeks he was named to the job.

It could not be said that Tom didn't know what he was getting into when he took on the challenge of managing Theatre Calgary. The desire to get in and do something had been a characteristic of his work as a volunteer. Now, when it was a question of a new career, Tom again opted for an active, hands-on role.

"Theatre Calgary had a terrible financial problem. They needed somebody who knew the city and could raise money or get people to help in raising money, and my old banking job gave me those key pieces of knowledge. When I took the job we were $2 million in the hole and now we are $750,000 in the black," he says with obvious and justifiable pride. "I didn't do it by myself. I had a wonderful team, and the staff quickly learned to understand the bottom line and plan our activities in a realistic fashion. It meant a lot of long days at the beginning, but now I have more freedom to play golf and enjoy myself."

Now that he is close to the age when he originally thought he would retire, Tom is showing few signs of slowing down. He serves on a few corporate boards and thinks he might like to increase the number of those assignments he takes on. He's also thinking that he'd like some more time for his non-work interests. "I would also like to be able to play more golf and do my photography, and woodworking and bridge playing—and then there is, of course, the Zoo." Tom is the volunteer chairman of the Calgary Zoo and has worked his magic there, raising its profile and substantially improving its financial position.

Tom is quietly confident that new opportunities will continue to find him. "I have talents that organizations can use—organizations are always looking for management experience, and people of 60 bring a great deal of that to the table." Fortunately, his many years with the bank left him in a position in which gainful employment is not a necessity but rather undertaken primarily for the enjoyment and fulfillment it brings. "I have taken a lot out of the world, and so now it's payback time. If I believe in an organization's objectives, I will gladly help to the best of my ability. It keeps me involved and alive and interesting."

Tom is working to blend his many interests and activities into a diversified and interesting lifestyle. He has no doubt that he can. But he's not considering "retiring" from Theatre Calgary anytime soon. "I know I just could not stop working. I would go crazy. I want time for me now, and I will want more of it as time goes on, but I also know I want and need to make a contribution."

Tom's belief in the value of working, even when you no longer need to work, has been influenced by observing friends and colleagues who "just stopped." They were completely at a loss when retirement arrived early. The road back to a productive life was not clear, and their physical and mental condition declined rapidly. Tom finds that tragic.

He offers this advice to younger high fliers: "Spend time preparing for the day you will no longer occupy the corner office. Don't think that, because you have an important job, you don't need to develop other interests. Remember that your employer doesn't own you. You can say no. Also remember that you may not get to choose the timing or the manner of your departure, so be prepared." His only regret about his own transition is that it might have been easier if he had spent more time getting ready.

There are some valuable lessons in Tom's story.

- Always have a second string to your bow. Just as you invest your financial wealth in a diversity of assets, invest your human capital in different activities. This is the best preparation for the unexpected.
- Develop passionate interests in your middle years. Then, when you achieve the freedom to choose how to spend your time in later life, there will be options you will be delighted to pursue.
- Contrary to what economists tell us, hard work is sometimes its own best reward.

SUDDEN AND COMPLETE

One day you are working; the next day you have no assigned work activities. The sudden switch may be harmful to your health. Unless you have planned just what you want to do and have taken the steps that are laid out later in the book, you may be spinning your wheels for some time while you cast about for something to fill the time your job used to require. This in turn can lead to boredom, ennui, frustration and a general decline in the perceived value of life.

One variation on retirement that has been gaining increasing popularity is a gradual phasing out of work and a gradual buildup of other activities. It is not so much a matter of taking longer vacations as of taking ever-longer weekends until you are finally down to one day's work each week. The transition to no days is then not so much an upheaval as a gradual transition. Some believe this form of phased retirement allows all the parties involved (including the retiree's spouse or partner) to become accustomed to the change in lifestyle and time usage that accompanies retirement.

There is, however, a need to address the payment—whether partial or full—of pension benefits. If, as the work week declines, so does the pay, with nothing making up the difference, then the income adjustment will be quite severe and probably discourage most workers from selecting such an option. The problem is not insuperable. It just requires flexibility.

THE PENSION FUND TRAP

In most private pension schemes, once you reach retirement age as defined under the plan, you cannot make further contributions to the plan. You are, in effect, being penalized because you do not receive the contributions the employer, prior to your retirement, made to the fund on your behalf. In some cases you are also required to take the pension. Even if you would prefer to work, you may well decide to retire.

Suppose, however, that you have the opportunity continue to work for the same employer beyond the retirement age, make no further contributions to the pension fund and defer your acceptance of the pension until some future date. Then you use your employment income to make the maximum contributions to an RRSP and perhaps save some additional amount, even though it is with after-tax dollars. If you delay the receipt of your pension, whenever you do begin to receive it, the expected payout period will be shorter. Moreover, your pension fund will accumulate additional investment earnings during your period of prolonged work, so the actual payout to you when you do receive it should be larger. And, because your employer made no contributions after your normal retirement age, the company comes out ahead as well. And the company continues to have the services of an informed, experienced and loyal employee.

If ever there was a win–win outcome, this is it. Yet companies steadfastly ignore this potential, either because they have failed to think it through or because they are dominated by an inherent age bias. This will and should change over time, as labour surpluses rapidly change into labour shortages. Intelligent employers are already considering what changes might be required. The more critical labour shortages become, the greater will be the temptation to sweeten the pie by allowing continued pension contributions after the normal age of retirement.

THE SPECIAL CASE OF THE CANADA PENSION PLAN

Most of us are so concerned about the simple viability of Canada's public pension scheme that we don't spend a lot of time thinking about what it means to us individually until we become eligible for benefits at age 60. Then we have a decision to make: take the pension as soon as possible, or wait while the value of the monthly payments grows by 0.5 per cent with every month of delay until age 70. As will be made clear below, for many TOTREPS (trade-off-talking rational economic persons), the calculations favour taking the pension sooner rather than later. There's just one catch—you have to cease working in the month you apply for the CPP if you are less than 70 years of age. Thus, although the CPP does reward continued participation in the workforce with higher benefits, this administrative rule has a disproportionate and often perverse impact on people's decision regarding when to leave the workforce once they reach the age of 60.

The rules also say that you can go back to work once the benefits start and—good news for both you and your employer—you don't have to make any further contributions. In other words, you can't both contribute and draw benefits at the same time. While this has a lot of charm if you are the employee or employer, one wonders what the government was thinking when it established the rules. The CPP is a "pay-as-you-go" plan—but the government doesn't want your contributions if you are receiving a pension benefit. Who made up these rules? Do they make any sense at all?

This brings us back to our first concern: the viability of the CPP. The issue needs to be considered from the point of view of the federal Treasury—even though this is a view most people are not used to taking. The reason this is important is that the greater the burden on the Treasury, the less likely the CPP will remain immune from detrimental change, especially if the workforce supporting it will be declining in size over the next 30 years.

The CPP Rules

- You can begin to collect CPP any time after your 60th birthday.
- At "normal" retirement age, 65, the maximum benefit in 2002 is $788.75 per month—a number adjusted annually to reflect inflation as measured by the consumer price index.
- Your pension is reduced by 0.5 per cent for each month prior to your 65th birthday that you claim it, to a maximum of 30 per cent.
- Similarly, it is increased 0.5 per cent for each month after your 65th birthday that you delay in claiming it, to a maximum of 30 per cent.
- Once you accept the CPP, you are no longer able or required to contribute to the plan, even if you are gainfully employed.

- Your benefits are subject to tax.
- Your contributions are matched by your employer and in total amount to 9.9 per cent of the first $34,800 of annual income.
- If your annual earnings are less than $3,500, you are not required to contribute.
- You must stop work in the month prior to receiving your first pension cheque, and you must apply for the pension to receive it.

To demonstrate what all this can mean to workers on the one hand and to the federal Treasury on the other, we have examined a range of alternative scenarios for a mythical person called Mike. What is common to all of them is as follows. Mike is single and, when working, earns $34,800 per annum, so he pays CPP on his entire salary. His birthday is January 1, and his life expectancy is exactly 81 years. (Well, he doesn't know this, but we have to assume a check-out date for the purposes of the analysis, so Mike gets his full four-score years plus one.) He lives in Ontario and is subject to the tax laws as of September 1, 2001, as they apply to a full-time resident of that province.[4]

Upon retirement, Mike will receive his CPP pension but no other income (so we are ignoring the Old Age Security and the Guaranteed Income Supplement), and he has not split his CPP benefits with anyone else (a former spouse, for example). At age 65, Mike will be eligible for the maximum amount of pension under CPP. Mike is in good health, likes his job well enough and is not counting the days until he can leave his employer. He wants to know if he should plan to retire at 60, as soon as he becomes eligible for CPP benefits at 60, or whether he should keep working until 65 or even 70. Here then are the results.

Option 1—Take the CPP at Age 60

Mike will receive a monthly cheque for 70 per cent of the maximum CPP benefit of $775 payable at age 65; he will get $542.50 per month, or $6,510 per year. The total payments over the next 21 years until age 81 will be $136,710. This stream of payments has a present value at age 60 of $77,626.76.[5] Because he elects to take the pension at 60, he and his employer pay no further premiums, but Mike has to get out of the labour force for at least one month.

Option 2—Take the CPP at Age 65

Mike will receive a monthly cheque of $775, or $9,300 per year; the total payments for the next 16 years, until age 81, are $148,800. This has a present value at age 65 of $95,509.47, and present value for the individual at age 60 of $74,634.81. However, there's a catch: to collect this higher amount, Mike will have to pay a CPP contribution of $141.45 per month for five years until he turns 65. To make the analysis truly reflect all the financial facts, Mike has to subtract the present value of those five years of additional payments into the CPP. Assuming the same discount rate, five years of those payments has a present value of $7,316.58, which has to be subtracted from the present value at age 60. This leaves a net present value of $67,318.23—that is, $10,308.53 less than Option 1.

Option 3—Take the CPP at Age 70

If Mike continues to work and waits to take the CPP until he reaches age 70, his monthly payment will be 30 per cent more than if he elects to take the pension at 65. He'll receive a monthly check for $1,007.50, or $12,090 per annum. The total payments over 11 years will be $132,990. This looks like a pretty good deal until he applies discounted cash flow analysis and discovers that, while the present value at age 70 will be $97,183.04, the present value of that stream at age 60 is only $54,266.50. Again, $141.45 must be paid monthly—for ten years this time—to obtain this amount. Subtracting the present value of the premiums, which is $12,740.89, leaves a net present value of only $41,525.61.

The decision is, as they say, a no-brainer. Mike should take the CPP and run! And now, consider that, if Mike retires at age 60, claims the CPP and then returns to work, and works until he turns 70, he will receive the CPP while he and his employer will be free of their combined 9.9 per cent annual CPP premium. Yes, he'll have to pay income tax, but he can reduce that by making a contribution to an RRSP until his 69th year—or until he ceases to have employment income. He can than draw down the RRSP, thereby supplementing his CPP pensions.

Mike, being a TOTREP, approaches his employer and says that, regretfully, he'll be leaving on his 60th birthday. The employer, reluctant to lose a reliable employee, lets Mike know that he can return to work after a six-week vacation—part time, if he prefers. Mike, who rightly thinks the CPP benefits aren't all that generous, agrees. He could use the extra income, and, after all, working isn't so bad. Both he and his employer are noticeably better off because there are no more CPP contributions to pay. Even better, Mike can now use his CPP income to fund an annual RRSP contribution for as long as he has employment income or until his 69th year. He can then begin to draw down that amount, exhausting it on December 31, just before his 81st birthday.

Such an arrangement is extremely attractive to both the employer and the employee. Even if the employer makes some modest contribution to the employee's RRSP, the cost would likely be less than continuing to pay CPP contributions. If you want to maximize the burden on the Treasury (and, as TOTREPS, most of us do), this is the way to do it.

In the above scenario, everyone wins except the Treasury. Let us, just for a moment, look at the issue from the point of view of a Treasury bureaucrat whose job it is to maximize Treasury revenues. This nameless, faceless bureaucrat wants us all to work continuously until age 70, paying our income taxes as well as our CPP contributions and only claim the CPP at 70. Yet, rational economics would lead us to conclude that anyone thinking about it would take the CPP at age 60 and then, if the opportunity is available, return to work for as long as he or she wishes and is able to do so. But what is good for the individual may not work for the entire country. With CPP contribution rates rising and the stability of the system in question, the Treasury bureaucrat needs to optimize revenues for the CPP so that it will be there not just for today's retirees but for tomorrow's. She realizes that encouraging people to retire and cease making contributions at 60 no longer makes any sense.

This evidently nonsensical situation exists because we have a public pension policy that was designed in part to deal with the problem of surplus—not scarcity—in labour markets. The CPP was originally intended to get people to stop work, even at the expense of forgone income tax and CPP contribution revenues. It's clear our national pension scheme needs an overhaul and needs it now.

Public policy should be aimed at encouraging people to work as long as they wish and are able to, and to defer receiving CPP benefits until they are ready to quit work on their own schedule. This would minimize the payout of the CPP. The way to do that is to change the current time indifference in how early or late claiming of the CPP is structured. What we should do is sharply increase the monthly payment the longer the individual waits to claim CPP. Obviously, when people decide to retire would then be a function of their life expectancy and the attractiveness that retirement holds for them. This is as it should be—though it is not so at present. At a minimum, the national pension scheme should be neutral. It should not push people into retirement before they are ready. Neither, in its own interest, should it encourage employees to arrange with their employers to claim the pension and discontinue the payment of premiums while they continue to work.

TAX TREATMENT OF TRAINING EXPENSES

Another barrier to working after age 65 can be the need for special training or retraining. But, if you are over 65 and need retraining, can you deduct the cost? During your "working years," any cost of training for a job or professional upgrading is tax-deductible. But don't try deducting your computer course or business writing seminar fees once you reach 65; training fees are a legitimate expense, but only before "retirement age." This in effect means that the cost of training goes up after age 65 by your marginal tax rate, and that may well put it beyond the financial capacity of a significant number of citizens. The Treasury's attitude on this question is that allowing for the deduction could result in abuse of the provision. The simple solution is to permit the full deduction of the training costs only against earned—not pension—income. If the Treasury is truly terrified of unleashing an army of pensioners desperate to consume training courses, they could even spread out the deduction over a number of years. Any residual amount left, should the person die before claiming all of the tax benefit, would revert to the estate of the individual. Again, looked at in the aggregate, the sums would not be huge but the flexibility this strategy provides to seniors is potentially enormous.

VOLUNTEERING AND GETTING RIPPED OFF

During their working lives, many community-minded individuals devote a considerable amount of their time to working as volunteers in the not-for-profit sector. Whether they volunteer with the Lions or the Rotary or the Red Cross, or coach little league baseball, volunteers are an important resource for many arts, sports, community service, education and health organizations across Canada. Many more citizens support these organizations with financial contributions but find that there just isn't time during their early and middle careers to give time as well as money.

In planning for retirement, many people look forward to volunteering more time to the worthy cause(s) of their choice. And, for those who can afford to be entirely without employment income, full-time or part-time volunteer "jobs" may be the ticket to a fulfilling and enjoyable retirement lifestyle. But what if you have the time and the commitment, but are concerned that your public or private pension income may be insufficient to assure you the standard of living you aspire to in retirement? You may feel that you just can't afford to volunteer as much time as you would like without any financial reward.

Consider, however, the benefits of volunteering as a means of supplementing your disposable income—as well as enhancing the life of your community. If that were possible, you would have the satisfaction of doing something you think worthwhile and the organization would enjoy the benefit of your services for free or for substantially less than true market cost. Calculated as the sum of the efforts of thousands of volunteers, the benefits to the not-for-profit sector and the people they serve could be immense.

How can this be done? Simple. Just change the tax law to allow the registered charity for which the volunteer works to issue to the volunteer a tax receipt in the amount of the minimum wage for the number of hours worked. That receipt in turn could be used to reduce the tax burden on retirement income, acting in effect as an income supplement. To prevent abuse, all such receipts would be subject to audit, and willful violation of the system would result in the immediate loss of the organization's charitable status. That should be an adequate deterrent if anyone is inclined to issue tax receipts for family and friends who don't provide documented volunteer work.

Consider how this simple change in the tax law might facilitate the adjustment of communities to changes in its industrial structure. David has a friend who was employed for years by a major manufacturing enterprise in Hamilton. With the advent of free trade, the plant was closed and operations were moved out west. David's friend was left with a minimum pension at the age of 56 and little prospect for employment. The friend had long been a pillar of his community. He served on the church board, coached minor league hockey and was elected to the school board, yet with the loss of his job his standard of living was sharply reduced. He and his wife could survive all right—but only just. He finally found a job at a much lower level of pay and with hours that essentially precluded much of his volunteer work.

Think how much better off he and his community would have been if this simple adjustment in the tax system had been in place. The total dollar amount of forgone tax revenue to the Treasury could be limited by restricting the deduction to people who had retired or who worked for pay for less than ten hours per week. The actual limit could be easily calculated on an individual basis, just like RRSP contributions.

A CALL TO ACTION

These barriers to allowing you to decide when, where and how you will change your working life need to be eliminated. Everyone reading this book can take some steps to help eliminate the barriers—both at the workplace and in public policy.

At work, ask your human resources department what alternative forms of retirement they offer. Ask why the company has a mandatory retirement policy (if it does) and whether they find it easy to hire replacements for the retirees who are let go each month. Ask them to explain how employee evaluation forms and procedures might have to be changed if retirement were no longer mandatory.

As a voter, you can write to your MLA and MP to ask why mandatory retirement is still permitted and why civil servants are offered a maximum pension based on years of service, in effect telling them to retire when their pension is maximized. During federal and provincial elections, ask the candidates in your riding where they stand on the issue of mandatory retirement. Ask them how their party will improve the benefits if workers wish to stay on past age 65. Ask them to support tax reform to improve the treatment of volunteer work and to extend the tax deductibility for retraining to any and all working Canadians, not just those under 65.

Finally, join Canada's Association for the Fifty-Plus (CARP), and encourage them to lobby to eliminate the barriers to working past the big 65.

Your 65th birthday is really no different from any other birthday before or after. Using that event as a watershed that limits your future activities makes no sense whatsoever. Each of us is unique, yet government and many of the institutions in the private sector assume that a host of changes suddenly transpire on that day for all of us. The real world doesn't work that way, and the system must be made to recognize and accommodate that fact.

If you are a Treasury gnome or an HR manager and you imagine the boomers will accept these constraints or barriers quietly, wake up! You are assuming that, when they approach 65, the largest and most vocal age cohort that Canada (and, indeed, the developed world) has ever seen will suddenly go to ground. And if you believe that, you're also ripe for sales pitches from Santa Claus and the Easter Bunny.

Chapter 5

Time for Yourself

Creating Your Personal Retirement Plan

THE NEXT THREE CHAPTERS deal with building your personal retirement plan. We're *not* talking about financial planning, but rather about the mental and psychological preparation needed for a happy and productive life after full-time work. If you have gained basic financial security, you will still face many choices about how you will use your time and talents to gain the intangible returns everyone wants out of life. You will need to make these choices wisely, using all your life experience to help you. And, if your personal financial circumstances require you to continue working after "normal" retirement age, you will need to plan ways in which you can adapt your working life to your changing personal priorities.

THREE STEPS TO YOUR PERFECT PLAN

There are three steps in the planning process we're proposing: self-assessment, answering the big questions and assessing your options.

Step 1—Self-Assessment

First you will need to do a personal inventory. You need to get to know yourself again, not as a young person trying to find his or her place in the world, but as a person with many years of valuable work and life experiences to draw upon. What are your likes and dislikes? What are your major strengths and weaknesses? Your experience will provide the answers if you review it thoroughly and honestly and with an open mind.

Step 2—Answering the Big Questions

When you've completed your personal inventory, you'll be in a good position to answer some of the big questions you will face as the traditional retirement age approaches: Should I change my work, or should I work at all? What do I want to do with my increased leisure time? Do I want to stay where I am or move to the city or the country or even another province or another country? How will my decisions affect those closest to me?

Step 3—Assessing Your Options and Setting Goals

Contrary to popular belief, your range of options concerning how you will spend your time may expand as you get older. This abundance results in a delightful dilemma: how do you choose among the various employment, volunteer or leisure opportunities before you? Just as research and networking were important in making career decisions in earlier decades, so they will now help you optimize the satisfaction you obtain from the activities you undertake "after work."

WHY PLAN?

A successful retirement is not something that just happens. From conversations with the people interviewed for this book, it became apparent that those who have had a rich and fulfilling life after the end of their full-time working lives thought deeply about what they wanted to do in their later years.

The period in your life from 60 on will make up a considerable chunk of your existence, so it makes sense that you would devote considerable thought and care to what you want to do with this portion of your life. Obviously you will want to make your "golden years" as rewarding, stimulating and pleasurable as possible. But, like career success, such a delightful outcome does not suddenly happen in a mysterious or miraculous fashion. While a few lucky so-and-sos may achieve both career goals and retirement goals without any visible effort, for most people there is a powerful link between their level of preparation and the results achieved.

Think back to your youth. You spent your first 18 to 22 years—or more—equipping yourself for life in the adult world of work and family responsibility. You had to acquire a variety of skills and competencies—as well as a bewildering array of social graces that your parents felt would smooth your way in life. The skill set you will require for the last third of your life may not take as long to acquire and may not be so broad in scope. After all, you can already speak, read, write and do cognitive reasoning—all skills you had to learn from scratch as a child. Nevertheless, you will have to devote some time and effort to preparing yourself to ensure that this next period of your life is what you want it to be.

Why is this? Surely the hard-won independence you have gained by fulfilling your employers' or clients' expectations for many years and saving diligently should in and of itself guarantee satisfaction with your life in retirement. After all, you can now set your own priorities and choose to undertake only those activities you enjoy. But there's the rub. With the freedom to choose comes a need to make intelligent choices that will yield the outcomes you want. The right choices for others may not be the right choices for you, and they may not be immediately obvious. Think of the simple soul who, when asked how he plans to spend his retirement, says cheerfully and succinctly, "Goin' fishing!" Does he really mean that every day, when he gets up and asks himself what he wants to do that day, the answer will always be "Goin' fishing"?

There is also the possibility that you may want to do things that require more than leisure and financial resources. Like advanced courses in university, they may have prerequisites. You may need to get a ticket stamped before you are able to participate. For example, suppose you really enjoy managing your own investments. You think you might want to take up advising others on assembling and growing their retirement nest-egg. You may, therefore, want to qualify as a registered financial planner (RFP). Something like this takes advance planning.

There's another way to appreciate the need for planning. Chances are that, in your youth, like many Canadians of your generation, you travelled quite a lot. You may have set off for

Europe with nothing more than a backpack, a rail pass and a list of youth hostels—and you probably had a great time. Now, think about the trip you planned for your 25th wedding anniversary. Did you buy several guidebooks or do extensive research on the Internet? Did you ask friends and colleagues for their personal recommendations? Did you spend at least ten minutes a day deciding where to go for dinner?

Somehow, as people amass experience in life, they gain insight into those kinds of experiences they find most rewarding. No longer is everything life presents equally exciting. They may find that they prefer the mountains to the seashore, vacation cottages with a complete kitchen to grand hotels with room service, the opera to a soccer match. Or vice versa. In any case, they know a lot more about their preferences and want to allocate their valuable time in ways that will provide the greatest psychic return. This takes planning too. Even if you think of retirement as a long vacation, you'll enjoy it more if you plan ahead now.

No one else can do the planning for you—though many of your friends and family members will be able to help. And it will take some time. There is no magic 15-minute questionnaire that requires you only to plug in your answers and wait a few minutes while the machine prints out—in double-spaced, large-type format—explicit instructions on how to achieve your perfect retirement.

Doing the work to think about your future will be time well spent. The evidence is overwhelming that those who enjoy the best health and the greatest amount of satisfaction in their daily lives are those who are mentally and physically active. The people who get the most out of life after 60 are those who are making a contribution to society and who are challenged to use all their faculties to the fullest. Life is a wonderful gift, and simply waiting to die is not a viable alternative. Living an active and interesting life in retirement may well be the greatest reward for a lifetime of work.

Now, if you still feel tempted to skip the planning process outlined above, just think for a moment of a friend or colleague who gave no thought to retirement and found himself cast adrift without any idea of what to do beyond playing endless rounds of golf.

LIFE IS NOT A GOLF COURSE: SHAUN BUTLER

Shaun Butler was 57 when he retired from a career in corporate marketing. After more than 35 years of increasing responsibility and rising workloads, he was looking forward to kicking back and spending time just relaxing. He would move to a beautiful new Cape Cod community on a golf course. He would do what he wanted to do when he wanted to do it. It sounded like the perfect description of paradise.

The only trouble was that it didn't quite turn out that way. After a few months, the thought of playing golf each day turned from pleasure into something approaching a burden. Shaun began thinking, Is this all there is? Is this what I have to look forward to for the next 20 or 30 years?

He tried broadening his horizons, getting into a program

of reading and learning how to surf the Internet—but these activities had their limits, especially because they were essentially solitary. And while golf still offered some pleasure, Shaun was missing the contacts with the wide range of people that his business life had provided—though he hadn't recognized the value of this perk when he was working full time. Now his life was focused on those in his immediate community and, as Shaun himself said, "The topics of conversation got down to three: who was sick, who had died and the weather." He was slowly going out of his mind.

The thought of going back into corporate life was not overly appealing. Organizations had been downsizing; this meant that holding a management job would involve even more intense work pressures than Shaun had experienced before retirement. Also, he felt he had done his duty in the trenches. He wanted mental stimulation but not the stress and long hours involved in corporate life.

Determined to take up a productive activity, he started working on a business plan to develop an advertising agency on Cape Cod, where he lived. Advertising was, after all, part of the skill set he had developed in his work life and, since he was interested in his community, it was a way of keeping his interests alive. After he had developed a draft plan, he decided to take his work to a friend who ran an agency in nearby Boston and who, during Shaun's business career, had been one of the suppliers to Shaun's former employer. He was looking for constructive feedback.

The head of the agency reviewed the plan and came back

to Shaun with an unexpected proposal. Rather than start a new agency, Shaun could come in as a partner in his firm. What the agency head needed was somebody who could take on part of the load and who could act as a marketing consultant for his customers. As Shaun said, "Many customers either knew they had a problem but didn't know how to fix it or didn't know they had a problem and needed to be told about it." The head of the agency knew that Shaun, as a former purchaser of agency services, could spot those problems a mile away and also knew how to fix them. Obviously, Shaun was just the type of guy with the skill set he was looking for. However, he also knew Shaun was retired and had said before that he was anxious to leave the rat race. Would Shaun be willing to get back in the business?

Indeed he would, but only under a set of conditions that would give Shaun the flexibility he wanted to allow him to pursue other activities he found attractive. No 60-hour weeks, but flexibility and a degree of choice regarding when and where he worked.

Now Shaun is a partner in the firm, helping clients with their marketing problems and enjoying himself immensely. He knows he is making a contribution to both his clients and the agency. The work has put him back in contact with a wide range of people.

There have, however, been some adjustments, as Shaun himself admits. "The trappings that were so important in the corporate world are now missing. I do a lot of my own administrative work, and those hours spent with the Internet have proven useful in finding information, setting up contacts and, if need be, booking reservations. But, I don't mind it."

Shaun, looking back on his initially unhappy adjustment, says he learned some lessons:

- Retirement is going to last a long time, and it warrants planning what you are going to do. While playing golf might sound attractive, you should also think about your current work life and what aspects of it give you pleasure. Think through how you can continue to experience those pleasures—perhaps in a different environment. You want life to be interesting, not just relaxing.
- Think about what skills you have developed during your work life and how they might be used to benefit both yourself and others once you have decided to leave your current work. Working after retirement should be primarily for pleasure, if you can afford it.
- If necessary, have the courage to admit that the way your retirement dream is unfolding is not what you imagined. Have the determination to find out the source of the problem, and then do something about it. Retiring does not mean that you have suddenly lost all of your analytical capacities. Rather, you have to learn to apply them to new and sometimes unexpected challenges.

THE IMPORTANCE OF SELF-ASSESSMENT

Setting up your plans for life after 60 should include a good dollop of dreaming—after all, you've earned the privilege of considering your personal desires, not only the goals of your employer or the needs of your children. But, to be really useful, your deliberations also have to be grounded in practicality. It is difficult to become a specialist in statistical methods if you do not like math, and it is difficult to become a participant in the senior Iron Man competition if you can neither ride a bike nor swim. Walter-Mitty–like fantasies have their place, but when you are planning your future, the most important inputs are the lessons of your own experience—which by now are probably legion.

So, realistic self-assessment is the cake, and a touch of dreaming is the icing; and both are best enjoyed in judicious proportions! Something of a stretch is possible, but remember that while everyone wants to exercise control over their futures and make the choices that are right for them and their partners, most people will also value a high level of continuity in relationships, lifestyle and interests. So you need to be realistic about what is possible in a financial and professional sense as well as about what it is that really gives you joy. But, who knows? Maybe doing something you have long had your heart set on is not impossible after all.

The exercise of identifying your retirement alternatives and making choices among them will be easier if you first take the time to make an inventory of your personal assets and preferences. By "assets" we don't mean the financial or real assets you have accumulated but your talents and special strengths—along with your weaknesses. We all have some. By preferences, we don't mean your favourite colour or whether you like red or white wine but your strong likes and dislikes. Do you enjoy solitary activities such as reading or research, or do you always work or play in a group? Do you prefer indoor activities to outdoor? Do you thrive on the buzz of activity in the city, or are you anxiety-ridden about traffic jams and air quality?

THE STORY SO FAR

An easy way to compile your personal inventory of assets and preferences is to think about your life until now and to make outline notes for your autobiography. (No need to worry about finding a publisher or offending family and friends; this exercise is just for your own use at this point!) What have been the highlights and the low points and, of all the things you have done, what are you proudest of? Why were these events important? Why do you take particular pride in some accomplishments but not so much in others? When were you happiest, and when were you particularly low? Can you say why?

Everyone compiles a personal inventory in a different fashion. Some people write out in great detail their life story and then review it for recurring themes. Others make lists and refine them over a period of time. However you assemble your inventory, it really is important to take the time to write out your thoughts and recollections. The written text will serve as a handy reference for composing your lists of strengths and weaknesses, your likes and dislikes. Also, writing something down calls forth a degree of clarity in thought and expression that is often absent in conversational speech. So, you really didn't like that first job after university that so impressed your friends and family? Force yourself to articulate why you weren't happy in your work, even though everyone else thought you should be on top of the world.

An important point to remember when writing your life history is that you are not doing it for posterity or even for your high school guidance counsellor. This is for you alone and, as Shakespeare said, "This above all, to thine own self be true." Yes, warts and all. Don't boast—just write down the facts. The superlatives you can add later if you decide to turn your manuscript into an outline for a best-selling autobiography. Right now the audience is just you, and no one is going to grade you on your work.

Include as much detail as you want because it may reveal facets of yourself that perhaps you never realized were important. When you can't think of anything more that you want to add, put your life history aside for a day or two. Then come back to it and review it with a critical eye. Ask yourself if you forgot or avoided something. Is it an important omission? The more inclusive and honest the document, the better the clues it can give to your true talents, the better it will help you to identify what really excites you and what you would rather not experience ever again.

Writing out your life story may seem to be a step you can skip—but please don't. After all, you *are* planning the rest of your life, and this is a task very much worth doing well. You need to take the time and muster the discipline to get it right. If you would like some help structuring this step, turn to Appendix A and follow the outline suggested there in Exercise 1.

HITS AND MISSES

Once you are satisfied with your written life history, use it to draw up a list of your talents and weaknesses, likes and dislikes. Unlike your personal history, this list should be brief and focused. What are your three or four or five most important talents? Did you find a glaring weakness or two? What are your biggest likes and most virulent dislikes? Your strengths and weaknesses will help define your range of practical alternatives; your likes and dislikes will help you determine which alternatives you want to pursue and which you can dismiss without another thought. So take the time to do this right. Your goal is to create a list of talents and weaknesses, likes and dislikes that will be useful to you as a frequent reference as you develop your plan. It should help you to evaluate options quickly and thoroughly as they come along. If you'd like to follow a set format, turn to Exercise 2 in Appendix A.

When David did this exercise, he treated writing down his life history as a kind of expanded résumé, including not just work experience but also important life experiences such as raising children and adjusting to different family and employment situations. Here's his short list of assets and preferences.

Strengths	*Weaknesses*
Strong teaching skills	Shy in crowds
Effective public speaker	Not good on details
Good cook	Sometimes not a good listener

Likes	*Dislikes*
Debating public policy issues	People who rely more on emotion than on reason
Good writing	Poorly presented arguments
Spending time with friends and family	Duty dinners and networking events
Classical music	Rock and roll
Libraries, museums, art galleries	Most sporting events

Here's an example of how the list can be useful. After his "retirement" from the bank, David was approached to run for political office both federally and provincially. David likes speaking in public but hates working a crowd—so he decided politics was out. A trade-off that might have been worth making when he was younger no longer seemed reasonable—at least not when there were other projects he was keen to work on.

SEEKING VALIDATION

Next you need to validate your list. By "validating," we mean checking it out to see how realistic you have been. Have you made a reasonable and rational list that demonstrates a mature understanding of yourself, or have you indulged in a little revisionism of your own life's experience to make the story more like a scenario for a movie? In other words, were you unintentionally trying to fool yourself?

The validation process is simple, but it should be demanding. Find three or four good friends who are not in your immediate family and who know you well. Tell them you would appreciate their help with your "life begins at 60" planning exercise, and emphasize how important it is that you get frank and honest feedback. You're asking them for help because of their friendship and knowledge of you. If your friends accept the task, be prepared to see yourself as you never have before. This is not an experience you are guaranteed to find entirely pleasant, but it is very important that your friends level with you. Surely firm friendship can withstand a little truth, no matter how trying it may be to learn that how we see ourselves is not always how others see us!

Ask your volunteers the following: Do they think your list of strengths and weaknesses is accurate? Did you forget something, or leave something out that you would rather not confront? Listen to what they tell you, and if you are uncertain, ask them to expand on what they are saying. Now is no time to be reticent. You are planning your future, and you need to start off with a sound foundation. Having listened carefully to their feedback, you may want to make some revisions and even ask your friends to review the revised list.

Then, *and only then,* should you discuss your list with your significant other. To ask for his or her feedback sooner (that is, before going to your friends to perform your reality check), may put your loved one in a difficult position. She or he may not agree with what you have listed as strengths and weaknesses and may be reluctant to confront you with reality. In that case, both your planning efforts and your relationship could be in hot water. Why risk it? As Shakespeare said, "The better part of valour is discretion."

Then, listen carefully to the person who will be your partner in your new life; he or she can be your most valuable support and sounding board. The knowledge and empathy your partner can continue to share with you will be needed in the future when you are discouraged or feel you have suffered a setback. And, in sharing the process with your significant other, you are building another bridge to ensure that your loved ones are included in your vision for the future.

Once your list has been validated, you have the single most important tool for planning what you want to do with this portion of your life. Now, you're ready to set up a broad strategy for your retirement—determining what balance you will set between productive work and leisure pursuits and deciding where you will live.

ROLLING WITH THE PUNCHES: ALCID AND GEORGE YELLE

Brothers Alcid and George Yelle come from a large French Canadian family. To their siblings, it seems they have always been extremely skilled with their hands. Alcid's ability with woodworking is legendary. George is equally gifted, but his talents are more along mechanical lines, in building and repairing motors and making broken machinery run smoothly again.

Alcid pursued a career in the RCMP, and he noted that most officers live, on average, for only five years after retirement. He had no intention of adding weight to that statistic. He was planning to keep active both mentally and physically and to live to a ripe old age and spoil his grandkids. (The grandchildren were as yet unborn, but with three daughters, he was confident he would eventually have at least one or two to spoil like any good grandparent should.)

He planned to make furniture, do a great deal of gardening and play a lot of golf—until he went with David one day to help tend David's bees. The beehives just fascinated Alcid, and when David accepted a job on the West Coast, Alcid agreed to take over the hives. Within a couple of years the pair of hives had expanded to almost forty, and Alcid had an agreement with the head of the local nursery and some other farmers to put his hives in their fields to help in the pollination of their crops. In turn, he would give them some honey as "rent." Alcid hit on the idea of putting his excellent honey into 250-millilitre bottles and wholesaling them to schools for their fundraising projects. After all, he thought, it would be better for the students to sell natural honey than chocolate-covered almonds. Four years after he left the RCMP, Alcid was one of eastern Ontario's major honey producers.

George, the mechanical wizard, was a senior technician

at the National Research Council, also known as the NRC. In one of the seemingly endless rounds of federal government cutbacks of the 1980s, the NRC declared George's unit redundant and George started looking for some suitable position elsewhere in government. Just as he was about to accept a post, the NRC offered him another job. While he was happy to remain at the NRC, the incident was a forcible reminder that these kinds of layoffs could happen again at any time and that perhaps it was time to think of developing an escape route to minimize the downside.

George and his German-born wife, Gisela, enjoy the outdoors and loved their cottage on a nearby lake. Was there some way to combine his love of the cottage life and the desire to put in place some safety net in case things turned down again at the NRC? Both George and Gisela are outgoing and pleasant; they meet people easily and make them quickly feel comfortable. So they hit on the idea of perhaps running some sort of summer resort. Within a short time, they had located and bought a fishing camp on a lake in Quebec, about 100 kilometres north of Ottawa. It was a bit primitive, but George reasoned that he could fix it up and perhaps start to attract families who might like to come and spend a week or two at a place where they could fish, swim and do their own housekeeping and cooking. Gisela, a trained bookkeeper, would spend the summer at the camp, and George would come up each weekend from May until October.

In the depths of winter, George and several of his brothers and friends would go up to the camp and cut ice and store it in the icehouse so that, come summer, there would be plenty to keep each day's catch fresh. And, in winter and spring, both he and Gisela would be taking reservations for the coming season. It was a way to make having a cottage pay. When retirement from the NRC finally arrived for George in 1994, he just moved up to the camp for the full summer season.

Circumstances changed abruptly for Alcid when he was diagnosed with Parkinson's disease. It meant he had to give up woodworking because he was no longer able to safely hold the chisel when working on his lathe. For a time, he could still keep the bees, though lifting the heavy supers of the hives filled with honey became increasingly difficult—so eventually that too had to be abandoned. Now, he spends more and more of his spare time arranging trips for fellow retirees who are members of his golf club. He enjoys planning the itinerary and making all the travel and accommodation arrangements. He has also become very involved in working for the Parkinson's Society, helping them organize support groups for those with the disease and raising funds through various events. The annual spring walk for Parkinson's has turned out to be a big event in the greater Ottawa community, and Alcid is now on the national executive of the society.

Alcid clearly believes that the key to a satisfying retirement is to find ways to employ both his interests and his God-given talents to help himself and his community. He still has the ramrod posture of a Mountie and the physique as well. He doesn't feel sorry for himself: he knows he is making a contribution and takes pride in helping his three daughters in various tasks while keeping his golf game, his curling and his hunting skills sharp. His pace may have slowed a bit—but just a bit. Life is too enjoyable for him to do anything but cherish every day.

George and Gisela are making similar adjustments. They have found that the business of running a summer camp is becoming more difficult. The number of families willing to travel to the wilderness for an extended vacation is declining, especially now that the kids have so many organized summer activities. American companies, once the source of many of the camp's bookings, are also cutting back on that sort of entertainment and employee perk. So George and Gisela are planning to sell the camp to be able to concentrate on a new activity that they find very rewarding.

Gisela has a friend in Germany who at one time was thinking of emigrating to Canada but changed his mind and went into the travel agency business at home. One day he called Gisela and asked if she and George would be willing to meet some of his clients who were coming to Canada for a vacation and escort them to the various tourist sights in Quebec and Ontario. Since Gisela speaks German and George is fluent in French, the German tourists had excellent guides who were able to make them feel at home in every part of Canada. That first trip led to others, including guiding Californians who wanted to experience winter—something eastern Canada can offer in abundance! Now George and Gisela anticipate that the guiding business will replace the fishing camp as their major activity and as a supplement to their retirement income. A special advantage of their new venture is that they can both travel to research other destinations to suggest to their colleague back in Germany.

George, like his brother Alcid, adjusts to the changing times and seizes interesting opportunities when they present themselves. He and Gisela have a straightforward and simple objective: to make the most of every day, enjoy what they are doing and accept those challenges that promise to be both interesting and rewarding.

Perhaps the most interesting thing about the progress of the brothers Yelle is their clear recognition that preparing for retirement from their first careers would involve developing new ventures that could offer both satisfying work and some additional income. In both cases, they eventually left their first careers behind and launched into projects that drew on their recreational interests and hobbies. Then, as changing circumstances dictated yet more change in their lives, they adapted—apparently seamlessly.

We wonder how their stories might have unfolded differently if the brothers Yelle had reached retirement age without having visions of how they wanted to live and plans for what they wanted to do. They were not compelled by economic necessity to find new ways of earning a living, and they could easily have chosen a less proactive approach. Whether the number of their years after traditional retirement age would have been fewer, no one knows. What they surely would be is less interesting and rewarding.

The lessons to be drawn from their experiences are numerous, but the following are the most important.

- Because change is constant and inevitable, one of the most important uses of wisdom is to learn to live with change—if not with enthusiasm, at least with acceptance.
- Since few of us can perfectly control the timing of our exit from our first career, it is wise to develop "another arrow to our bow," as George did. If this alternative is also an activity that we one enjoy and profit from, so much the better.
- Although you certainly cannot anticipate or prevent a blow of fate such as Alcid experienced with Parkinson's, you can use skills of adaptation to lessen its impact on your ability to enjoy life and contribute to your community.

Chapter 6

Building a Framework

Answering the Big Questions

BEFORE WE TALK ABOUT the nuts and bolts of creating a retirement plan—one firmly rooted in knowledge of yourself and therefore uniquely suited to you—let's frame some of the big questions about your future. You will need to think about them and discuss them with those closest to you. The answers to these questions will create a framework within which you will be able to identify and assess your options for a satisfying life.

In this chapter, you are going think about the basic questions of where you want to live and how you want to spend your time. You will, of necessity, make compromises and trade-offs, so it's very important to determine what the most important considerations are for you. Is it important for you to be close to your grandchildren in another community or to stay in the same neighbourhood or city where you have a circle of friends and organizational involvements? Do you want to maximize your future income or make sure you have lots of free time for travel and other leisure pursuits? Do you prefer a benign climate or proximity to cultural amenities? Do you want to take time—finally—to become expert in a field that has always interested you or to "give something back" by volunteering your existing expertise in a cause you believe is important? Each of us makes these trade-offs according to our own lights; there is no "correct" choice.

Years ago, a wise career counsellor told Diane that in making key life decisions about where she wanted to live, what she wanted to do for a living and how much income she wanted to earn, she had to be prepared to compromise on at least one of these variables. In other words, a newly qualified doctor might decide to build his practice in small-town Canada in order to raise his family far away from the dangers and distractions of the city; but, in choosing life in the slower lane, he would give up the ability to match the income he might earn in a large city. Professional athletes, even though they might make millions per year, do not always get to live in the city of their choice. Mining engineers most often do not live in big cities but rather in those remote places where gold or other valuable mineral deposits are still to be found. Professional musicians, unless they are among the tiny group of internationally known soloists, do not usually earn a large income; and, if they are famous, they normally spend a great deal of time travelling from concert to concert.

So, the young person planning a career has to make decisions—though they are often made by default—about major trade-offs: for example, whether they want to sacrifice income for quality of life or whether they wish to subordinate progress in their career to a desire to remain geographically close to parents, siblings and high school friends. Of course, some rare individuals do manage to arrange all three factors—location, vocation and income—to their satisfaction for much of their working lives, but this is very unusual. (Canadians could be forgiven for believing more than most in this particular vision, since successive federal and provincial governments have devoted endless tax dollars to subsidizing wages, propping up dying industries and encouraging people to stay in communities that have lost their economic base.)

Now, how does this relate to planning for a happy and productive retirement? The fact that you have accumulated a number of years of experience and a six-figure RRSP does not mean that you can escape the important task of making trade-offs. You may find that, with the mortgage paid off, the kids safely degreed or certified and a realization that professional standing is just not as important to your self-image as it used to be, you have many more acceptable choices than you did at 30 as to how much income you require and about the type of title that appears on your business card. If you are in the very fortunate position of having enough pension entitlements or enough savings to support the lifestyle to which you aspire through age 100 without earning another loonie, you have a very wide range of choices regarding where you live and how you spend your time.

Perhaps you find that some external constraints on where you live can now be relaxed. You may have stayed in a city you found less than exciting for the sake of a spouse's career or to ensure that the kids could go to university with their friends. Now you find that you have a long list of places you would rather be—but what are the costs and benefits of uprooting and setting up a home in a new location?

Decisions about work, leisure and location are of course closely linked and, to some degree, interdependent. For clarity's sake, these issues will be discussed one by one.

What Role Does Work Play in Your Vision of an Ideal Life from 60 Onwards?

It's most important to approach this question with an open mind. Work is intrinsically neither good nor bad, and no one can say whether you "should" or "should not" work. But work is a way of securing both tangible and intangible benefits: money, of course, but also mental stimulation, contact with people with similar interests, a structure for the day, a respected role in the community. You need to think about your requirements for all these things when you think about whether work has a role in your retirement plan.

The other important thing to remember is that the nature and the structure of work are changing. No longer is it necessary to define the work you choose to do within the narrow confines of the employee's 40-hour week. There are many more choices, from self-employment to part-time contract work to volunteer work. You will have much more choice than did retirees of even a decade ago. In fact, today's 50-year-old may find at 60 that he or she faces more attractive career options than ever before. A reasonable goal for a rounded retirement plan should therefore be to attain both the basic financial security and the self-knowledge to make choices wisely among those options.

Try thinking about work in terms of time allocation. Perhaps 40 or 50 hours of work each week is too much, but 8 hours of work is too few. Perhaps a reduction in the work week over time would appeal to you? So again, you need to ask yourself a number of questions: Do you want to leave paid employment altogether? Do you want to stop work cold turkey, or would you prefer a gradual phase-in of more leisure over a period of time? Would a staged cutting-back be possible, given your current job and employer? Would you like to continue doing the work you do now if you could change your hours or responsibilities somewhat? Or do you just want to continue in the same routine?

Perhaps economic factors mean that you have no choice but to continue to work. If so, can you continue doing your current job, or would you like to change some aspects or your role—such as reducing your work week to four days instead of five, or changing your mix of responsibilities to emphasize the tasks you enjoy most? Can you envision any changes that would make more of a pleasure out of a practical necessity? If so, how can you convince your employer that these changes will be good for your organization as well? If you need to work but are facing mandatory retirement, do you have a plan that isn't going to dissipate your life savings by spending them on lawyers' fees?

Perhaps you're ready for dramatic change and there's a career option you've always wanted to explore, but you've never had the freedom before to take a flyer on something new. If it's now or never for that secret ambition, what does realizing it require in the way of special training or new skills? Do you want to dedicate the time and resources required? Trying to become a neurosurgeon after 30 years as a stockbroker may not be practical—but becoming a career counsellor or a lay preacher in your church might be well within the realm of possibilities.

DIFFERENT SCHOOLS OF THOUGHT: KEN FIDDES

For more than 35 years, Ken Fiddes was involved in primary school education. He was an administrator and a teacher of grades 3 to 6. "I really liked teaching children of that age," he says. "They are open to learning and eager to do so and, if you do it right, you instill in them a love for learning that lasts a lifetime. So in that sense it is very rewarding."

Ken never gave much thought to what he would do once he reached the mandatory retirement age of 65. He has always been keen on physical fitness, though, and concerns about maintaining a healthy diet led him to eat a great deal of fish. The proprietor of the fish store he frequented in Maple Ridge, B.C., used to ask him what he planned to do once he retired. He'd reply, "Oh, I plan to travel and keep running."

Not too long after he retired from education, Ken found that he was getting bored. As it happened, his friend the fish store operator was going off on a long vacation. Although he had found a substitute to manage the store, additional reliable help would be needed. Was Ken interested? Ken, having nothing better to do, said yes.

He stayed on after the fish store owner came back from vacation and, over the next year or so, he learned the fish trade: what to buy and where to buy it, how to dress a fish, what sold and what did not. He also became familiar with some of the pitfalls in the industry. With a highly perishable product, knowing your market and your customers' likes and dislikes and the extent of their willingness to experiment is very important.

Then opportunity knocked. The nearby town of Port Moody (a rapidly growing suburb of Vancouver) was, in the opinion of both Ken and the fish store owner, underserved in terms of a retail fish market. There was an opening for a branch in an attractive new residential and commercial development that eventually would contain more than 500 high-rise units within one block of the suggested store location. It was the mid-1990s, and British Columbia was booming. What could go wrong?

Ken's associate had a brother who already had a seafood restaurant in Port Moody; he also sold a modest amount of fish out of the location. Having his brother move into the market was not acceptable. Ken decided that he would go ahead on his own and open the store. "The opportunity as it appeared then was just too good to pass up. I know it was risky for a man over 65 to put his life savings on the line and to borrow a large amount of money, but I felt confident—and I still would today, if the conditions were the same as in 1996."

The only trouble was that things did not remain the same. The province's economy, to put it in technical terms, tanked, and the rest of the condominium project was put on hold.

The potential market suddenly stopped growing at its previous dizzy pace. New competition appeared in the form of expanded seafood departments in the local grocery stores. Another fish market opened, aimed at the large number of recent Chinese immigrants who now constitute a large part of the population of the Port Moody/Coquitlam region. Nevertheless, Ken's reputation for quality products and friendly service, as well as his willingness to experiment with new marketing ideas, kept things going. Recently, the local economy has begun to turn around, more of the planned condos are being built and the market seems to be growing—slowly, but growing. Ken has also recently faced a bout of prostate cancer, which he has survived with his sense of humour intact.

Ken still gives the same cheerful greeting that has become the hallmark of his store. His fish is still the freshest to be found, and his small lunchtime bistro is attracting a following with its stellar fish chowders. The traits that made Ken an outstanding teacher are obvious to his growing group of customers. He is more than willing to tell you about the characteristics of the various kinds of fish he sells and how each might be cooked. And he waxes enthusiastic about the value of fish in a healthy diet. The fish store venture may not have unfolded in just the way he had in mind, but he is doing something that he thinks is worthwhile.

Would he advocate greater planning than he did, for others faced with mandatory retirement? "Sure I would do some more thinking—I am reluctant to call it planning. At least it wouldn't hurt." The bottom line is that Ken considers himself lucky to have found something he loves as much as teaching.

Ken's story is a fascinating one. Clearly, Ken has the soul of an entrepreneur. Starting a new business after retirement is a challenge that many of us would find just too risky, but Ken is proof that it can be done and that it can produce many rewards—and not only financially.

Let's draw a few lessons from Ken's experience.

- If you're thinking of starting up a new business in a field unrelated to your first career, consider getting some hands-on experience in someone else's shop first. Not only can you learn a lot about the nuts and bolts of the trade, but you can also find out—at little cost to yourself—whether you really enjoy the business or not.
- Risk is something we all have to live with throughout our lives; it can be mitigated but never eliminated. It may be that a long career in a low-risk job with a good pension can be an excellent base for assuming the risk inherent in a business start-up—if you are blessed with an optimistic outlook and the nerve of a canal horse.
- Whether it's highly remunerative or not, the most important thing about your new career in retirement is that you enjoy it and feel that you are making a contribution.

Many books are available that dispense investment and financial planning advice, and this book will not attempt to duplicate their efforts. Suffice it to say that there are various reasons why you might want to earn an income in your retirement years. Your pension or savings, even along with CPP and Old Age Security, may be inadequate to the lifestyle you wish to maintain; this is quite likely to be true if you are single—especially female and single—or if you have been in the labour force for fewer than 30 years or if your choice of career was never designed to make you wealthy in the first place. And, even if you have a perfectly adequate retirement income from pensions or RRSPS (usually defined as 70 per cent of what you earned while working full time on a before-tax basis)—you may want additional income to save for your grandchildren's education (tuition fees are going up in most provinces!), to take an extra vacation each year or just to indulge your passion for collecting art, tasting fine wine or partaking of another of life's civilized pleasures.

Finally, you may simply want a paycheque as evidence that your skill or expertise continues to command a good price on the open market. There is nothing wrong with this. You are not taking a career opportunity or a chance to earn a good livelihood away from younger people. You are not depriving some bright young thing of a promotion. You are making a valuable contribution to an economy with an increasing shortage of skilled labour, and you are paying taxes on your wages to support health care, education and a host of other social goods you want for yourself, your children and your community.

There are many other ways to validate your individual worth—and many argue that the love of your family and friends and the respect of your peers should be at least as fulfilling as the payment for your professional services. But if your ability to earn is important to your self-esteem, by all means continue to earn, even if you give every penny to your favourite charity. Just keep in mind that the day may come when illness or disability or a change in market conditions may reduce your ability to earn and that neglecting your grandchildren for work makes no more sense at 70 than neglecting your children for work did at 35.

How Much Leisure Time Do You Really Want, and How Do You Want to Spend It?

This is the complementary question to those posed above about work. After all, time not dedicated to work is, by definition, leisure time. And this is the area where soon-to-be retirees expect the greatest change. Remember that full-time work, including commuting, occupies about 2,500 hours of a given year, so if you stop work cold turkey there will be a great deal of time to fill. It's worth repeating: after reading the newspaper, doing the breakfast dishes, putting out the garbage and walking the dog, about 2,000 hours will remain to be filled. Treat those hours as a special resource to be husbanded and used in the best way possible—to provide you with pleasure and stimulation—not just as hours to be passed in no particular way.

CLIMBING EVERY MOUNTAIN: PADDY SHERMAN

Paddy Sherman was a journalist for more than 46 years. His final position was as head of the Southam newspaper chain. When he retired at 61 in 1989 and returned to Vancouver from

Toronto, he had no carefully-thought-out plan for retirement. He did know one thing, however. What he had loved about Vancouver and British Columbia when he and his bride first arrived on the train after immigrating to Canada decades earlier was the mountains. "There were lots of them to climb, and that is what I loved doing—climbing." Therefore, retirement meant more time for climbing.

Paddy is in remarkable shape for someone in his 70s. But that has always been a characteristic of this wiry, good-humoured and very bright individual. Each week he does more than 10,000 vertical feet. By that, he means he climbs that height each week. One of his training grounds is the Grouse Grind, a steep mountain trail in North Vancouver that leads from a parking lot to the top of Grouse Mountain, the ski hill that overlooks Vancouver. Paddy can do the 2,700 feet in well under one hour. "It's good exercise before breakfast."

Back in Vancouver, his first task—aside from some modest part-time work as the chairman of Pacific Press and membership on the board of the Vancouver Aquarium—was learning how to ski. In a short time, he was skiing downhill racing courses; then it was on to extreme skiing classes. (Paddy notes that this does not mean jumping off cliffs but rather skiing on slopes away from the groomed runs.)

Of course, Paddy kept climbing mountains and doing mountain treks in Asia and South America. And Maureen, his wife of 50 years, persuaded him to build her a 16 x 20 foot guest cabin on the property they own on Galiano Island, in the Strait of Georgia, east of Vancouver Island. It took time, but Paddy had plenty of that. He took night-school classes, then built the cabin all by himself, including raising the side frames, using mountain climbing gear and his car. "I just used pulleys and tied ropes to the car bumper, which I backed up, thereby raising the frame. Simple."

He still reads avidly. "One of the things that you do as a newspaper man is read. You read your own paper and the competition and just everything in order to understand and to gain context. Reading keeps my mind alive, keeps me thinking and gives me balance with my physical workouts." Moreover, as a Fellow of the International Press Institute, he still goes to annual meetings around the world, where he not only renews old friendships but also sharpens his mind with the topics being discussed. He also serves on the Advisory Committee of the Media and Peace Institute; he was lured into this activity by his old friend Keith Spicer, who served as editor-in-chief when Paddy was the publisher of the *Ottawa Citizen*.

For Paddy, finding a balance in life is and always has been important. "I was never one to spend every waking moment on my work. I wanted to keep myself fit, and I wanted and needed time with my family. Luckily I was able to achieve that and enjoy my work. I loved being a journalist, but it was not my entire being."

Recently, his 12-year-old grandson asked Paddy to show him some techniques of rock climbing. "He is a youngster who is very proficient in climbing walls in the recreation centre in his community, but he suspected that rock climbing was somehow different. We went out last weekend, and he loved it. In fact, so much so that this summer the two of us are going into the mountains to spend a week just climbing." Listening to Paddy, you wonder who is more excited about the prospect: grandfather or grandson.

"I have never been a big long-range planner," Paddy admits. "I just took things as they came over the horizon, and I have found that to be true in retirement as much as during my working life. I have a host of projects that keep me busy. I am physically fit and intellectually alive. I enjoy every minute I am alive and feel fortunate that I have my health."

Unlike a lot of the case studies in this book, Paddy's retirement did not involve launching a new career. Rather, he chose to build on fitness and recreational interests to bring structure to his new-found leisure time. What conclusions can be drawn from Paddy's experience?

- Try to achieve a lifelong diversity in the things you do. Understand which activities provide you with pleasure, and make sure you have ample opportunity to pursue them.
- Try new things that build upon your existing enthusiasms. Paddy mastered skiing as a way of getting extra months in winter among the mountains that he so lovingly climbs in the summer.
- Keep your mind as well as your body challenged. Never stop learning. Never stop thinking.

Do you have hobbies to pursue or a long list of exotic places to visit or a gaggle of grandchildren to spoil? How much time do you want to spend on each? Be honest with yourself. If you've never made a bookcase, are you really going to take up serious cabinetry? If you're happiest in your own backyard, foreign travel may be glamorous but it probably won't be a lot of fun. If you can't stand the thought of visiting Disneyland, maybe you shouldn't plan to take the grandkids there. Besides, most people's grandkids lead pretty busy lives themselves these days.

It is quite uncommon for people to take up completely new leisure pursuits in retirement. Although your plan to take up quilting or cross-country skiing—even though you've no experience at either—may prove successful, it's just not very likely. If you think you'd like to spend a significant amount of time on a new hobby in retirement, try it now. Yes, it takes time away from work or from quality time with friends and family, but it is an investment in your future that is just as real as your RRSP contribution.

There's another important point to be made about leisure time. Just like fine wine, it is possible to have too much. The enjoyment of each unit of additional leisure may decrease, just as the third glass is not as rewarding as the first. Economists call this phenomenon "declining marginal utility," and it is always a signal to change direction and put your time and effort into something else that will provide a better return.

So, let's look at the time-allocation question again. If the thought of endless leisure hours to fill scares you (and, frankly, it scares most people who are accustomed to days filled with structured activities), the most straightforward solution is to allocate some of those hours to a productive activity: volunteering for a favourite charity, looking after the grandkids while their mom is at work, or even getting a job.

Are You Going to Move?

One of the biggest questions faced by many of the "soon-to-be-retired" is the question of where to live. It's also potentially explosive, because it is closely related to other decisions about work, leisure and lifestyle. It can be the source of much marital strife if the partners have differing views on the desirability of moving or about the destination or the schedule. Disagreements can also arise about how much of the family's financial assets should be tied up in real estate.

There are many factors to be considered, both for the individual and for the partners. How will a move assist in or disrupt your plans for work or leisure? Do you and your spouse simply want to downsize and free up capital, or are you truly ready to leave your province or even your country and start again in a new community or country?

Moving is difficult at any time of life. Even those who have moved frequently in their lives—wives of executives in international corporations and children of armed forces personnel, for example—enumerate the high costs: the disruption of friendships, interruption of school schedules and neglect of the "trailing" spouse's career. Then there are the challenges of making new friends and establishing new routines in each new place.

Having said all this, the allure of the new and different—or the nostalgically familiar—remains, and the ability to move to greener pastures is an important part of the retirement dream for many people. There is also the fairly common situation of the 50-something couple who have raised their family in a middle-class home in one of the country's hot real estate markets and find that its value has increased tenfold over 20 or 25 years. They realize that a tidy retirement nest egg can be theirs if they sell the family home and downsize—or move to a less expensive city.

For Canadians who want to relocate when they no longer have to live where their job is, there is an extraordinarily wide range of attractive choices—even leaving aside the possibility of escaping snow permanently in Florida or Arizona. Real estate developers are busy creating adult condominiums in city centres to appeal to empty-nesters who want urban amenities without the commute from the suburbs. Resort communities planned around golf courses for the "active retiree" are springing up in scenically gifted areas. Even whole towns are reinventing themselves as retirement communities, most often after the collapse of their former primary industry. Among those towns are Elliot Lake in Ontario, Miramichi in New Brunswick and Gold River on Vancouver Island. They offer inexpensive homes and organized activities geared to the retiree.

If you have decided that you want to work full or part time, this decision will likely influence your choice of location. Your line of work may limit where you can live if you want to continue in that work. If all your professional contacts are in Toronto and you want to build a part-time consulting practice, you probably won't want to move to Victoria, even if there is much less snow to shovel (and you could just hire someone else to do the shovelling).

On the other hand, e-mail and high-speed Internet access have revolutionized work flow for everyone from designers to financiers, and it may be that all you really need in a new location is easy access to a large airport. When we were deciding on a retirement property, we adopted rule 737: "If a Boeing 737 can't land there, we shouldn't live there."

How Will the Changes in Your Work and Leisure Priorities Affect Those Who Are Closest to You?"

This is probably the most important question of all to answer honestly. Are you blithely expecting a spouse or partner to adjust to your new priorities, or have you considered whether he or she has interests, concerns and obligations that will constrain what you might do as a couple? For example, your significant other may have a job he loves and may therefore be unable to take off for extended periods of time to travel, or he may be unable to move to your desired new location for several years. Or she may have developed particular community or volunteer interests over a substantial period while you were off conquering the business world, and she may be loathe to give them up just to accommodate *your* changed circumstances. If one of you participates in the annual garden show, extended travel during the growing season may be limited.

In any person's life, a major change in work or living conditions can be stressful for that person or for their families. Many a supposedly solid marriage has suddenly come apart when a crossroads was reached, especially if one of the partners reacted as if deciding on a new direction was a one-person show rather than a team effort. Those closest to you should not be made to suffer unintended collateral damage because you neglect to take *their* aspirations into account when planning for *your* retirement. Taking the care, time and thought to include them in charting out the impacts of your changed status on the family unit just makes sense.

The next step in determining the parameters of your future life will be setting some concrete goals and formulating some specific plans, such as a plan to travel for two months a year, or a goal of completing a course of study at the local university, or a plan to help the local library expand its operations. The goal could even be to launch a new business. Unless you are trying to qualify for official designation as an insensitive boor, making plans and setting goals in frequent and close discussion with the persons who will be most intimately involved is the wisest course. When both partners "buy in," then it is more likely that you will achieve the goal or implement the plan. As basketball great Michael Jordan once said, "TEAM is simple. It means Together Each Achieves More."

Chapter 7

Making Choices and Setting Goals

NOW IT'S TIME to think concretely about what to do and where to go to put your talents and interests to best use. This should be more fun than hard work. Now that you've done the inventory of your strengths and weakness, likes and dislikes and have determined the basic outline of a plan for the years ahead, you're in a position to evaluate your many options in terms of how they will contribute to your health, happiness and overall well-being and, just as importantly, to that of your family. What activities will best allow you to achieve your goals and provide you with pleasure and a sense of accomplishment? If you want to follow our format for creating your list of preferred activities and goals, see Exercise 3 in Appendix A.

If formal retirement is just around the corner, you might decide you want to continue doing what you have been doing while gradually reducing the amount of time you commit to it, thus leaving more time for travel or reading or golf or whatever attracts you. Or you might decide you need some further education or training. Or you might begin to collect information on businesses that you think would be able to use your services as an independent consultant.

This is the really interesting part—researching your options and making the choices or trade-offs. Even if your friends and colleagues consider you the guy or gal who "has it all," you will have to make some trade-offs. You cannot be everywhere and do everything all at once. But you can start by making a list of the specific goals you would like to achieve and the activities you would like to pursue as possible outlets for your energy.

AN ORDERLY RENEWAL: JIM GRAY

Jim Gray is a geologist by training. He likes order and precision in everything he does, and that is why he planned his progress from CEO into retirement almost to the minute. He devised a schedule (see Figure 6) under which he would gradually surrender management responsibilities in the company he had founded in 1971. As he gradually relinquished his management role, however, he planned to allocate more and more time to his many other interests, especially to not-for-profit organizations active in education and public policy. As Jim is fond of saying, he designed a process of renewal, not retirement.

Jim's company, Canadian Hunter Exploration, is a participant in the oil sector but is primarily known as a major producer of natural gas. From its beginning in the 1970s, Jim and his company have been good corporate citizens, supporting and participating in a variety of community-based activities.

Figure 6: **JIM GRAY'S TIME ALLOCATION CHART, 1995–1998**

source: Urban Futures Institute

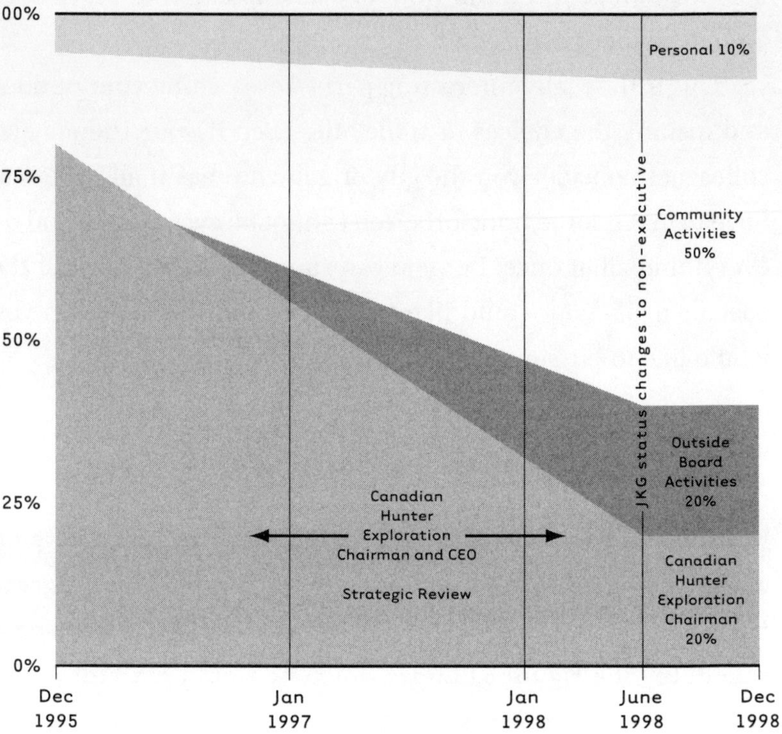

As a volunteer, Jim had headed the Calgary Economic Development Association, the local YMCA and the Canada West Foundation (a public policy think tank based in Calgary), and had served as chairman of the World Petroleum Congress when it met in Calgary in 2000. Given the volunteer track record Jim had established while still working full time, there was no shortage of organizations eager to enlist his considerable leadership skills as his work schedule became less demanding.

Jim is also a person of strong opinions. He has always considered it prudent to prepare for the future, and he has always believed that one of his major responsibilities to the shareholders of his company was to plan for an orderly management succession. He had seen too many examples of founders who clung to their positions, made no provision for succession and, when they left, put their companies, their employees and their shareholders at unnecessary risk. Jim made it clear to the company's stakeholders that he expected to decrease his involvement, groom a successor and leave all of his day-to-day management responsibilities behind by the time he reached his 65th birthday. He would continue to serve as a non-executive chairman.

Beginning shortly after his 60th birthday, Jim followed a carefully worked out schedule for relinquishing responsibilities. The slack in his packed schedule was taken up with more volunteer work in a host of different organizations in Calgary. He also began accepting more of the offers to serve on other corporate boards that had been coming to him with increasing frequency. Jim also made sure that everybody in his company knew about his schedule so that there would be as little uncertainty as possible surrounding the transition.

Outside the company, Jim became somewhat of an evangelist about planning for retirement—not in the financial sense, but in the sense of finding and developing interests that would provide a focus of activity and interest as work became less important. "Retirement will not be just a short-term venture," he says. "Plan on it lasting a goodly amount of time, and if you want to get the most out of it, then you have to devote care and thought to what it is that you want to do when you no longer have to follow a set schedule, when you no longer have someone else setting the schedule. Now you are in control of your time, and the priorities you set are your own, not someone else's. That, for me at least, was something new and I wanted to make sure that every day counted. There were lots of challenges and opportunities, and I wanted to put my energies and abilities to work on them. I wanted to make more of a contribution to my community and my country, and with good health and good fortune I will be given that opportunity."

At 67, Jim is enjoying each day of his "renewal." The schedule is still jam-packed, though the sale of Canadian Hunter Exploration in 2001 means that he is even more free of company commitments. He is currently serving on a number of corporate boards, though volunteer activities now consume the lion's share of his time. He reads voraciously—he's still learning. And he still enjoys every minute of every day, from his daily morning swim to the final paragraphs of his current "read" just before sleep.

It would be easy to dismiss Jim's experience as simply not very relevant for most people. After all, most readers of this book are not captains of industry. Most do not face the challenge of succession planning in the company they founded. And not all have the luxury of choosing the method and the timing of their departure from corporate life. But, there are some useful lessons here nonetheless.

- Everyone around you—your family, your employer and those who work with or for you—will benefit if you accept the inevitability of change and prepare for it. Recognizing that your choices will affect others and ensuring that you communicate your plans and expectations to others is an important part of your duty to the next generation. And, if you happen to be a captain of industry with employees and shareholders depending on you for their well-being, it is important to reduce the uncertainty these people face as a result of your life transition as much as you can.
- Even if you have an extremely absorbing career, developing outside activities that reflect the full breadth of your interests while you are still working will help you structure your plan for retirement. Then you will truly be retiring *to* your next career rather than *from* your job.
- Thinking of your transition to retirement as a process of renewal has tremendous psychological benefits. The transition becomes a beginning as well as an ending, providing new challenges and new goals that help you move forward. Since going backward is not an option, this can be a very good thing.

CREATING YOUR OWN GOALS

Diane, who is trying to rebalance her work life with her other interests, has a list of goals that currently looks like this:

Major Goals

1. Get involved with the performing arts again. (But not as a professional manager!)
2. Complete a transition from manager to part-time consultant to the business she founded in 1995.
3. Turn the backyard into a small but beautiful garden.
4. Travel to a new foreign destination each year.

Short-term Goals

1. Take a course in Excel and Word and other useful computer applications.
2. Finish decorating the guest suite.

Once you have a preliminary list of your own goals, you'll need to do some in-depth research on the alternatives that involve venturing beyond your actual experience. Start by asking your friends, family members and people whose judgment you respect where they think you could best put your talents to use. It would also be useful to do some independent research.

A raft of Internet sites cover every retirement-related subject and virtually every locality on the face of the earth. An annotated list of such sites appears in Appendix B of this book. You, limited only by the length of time you want to devote to it, can find all sorts of information here. Sorting through the list to select what's relevant to you may take some time, but you should be able to narrow a list down to something less than ten to add to your "bookmarks."

What Do You Want to Do?

This is both the best and the worst question of all—because it has so many possible answers. Having thought about your priorities, what can you do to participate in all that life has to offer, particularly if you have more time that you can call your own? What activities will most easily relate to your talents, preferences and priorities?

Review your list of possibilities by examining each of the alternatives and asking yourself these questions:

1. What makes this activity a good fit with my personal priorities, strengths and preferences?
2. What can I bring to this activity, and what will it bring to me?
3. How will I judge if this was a good choice for me? What things will confirm my choice, and how certain can I be that I will have the information to provide that confirmation?
4. How would I rate this alternative, compared with the others I am considering? Why would I rate it this way?
5. What might the possible downsides be, if any? What am I risking if I select this alternative?

What you are really doing in asking these questions is eliminating uncertainties. Taking some time to deal with uncertainties is always worthwhile—though you won't be able to eliminate all of them. The good news is that the risks inherent in making choices at this stage of your life are not likely to be as great as they were in your early career. Remember your first job interview? Perhaps you were extremely anxious about securing the "right" job to give your slim résumé some of the heft it needed. Recall the anxieties you experienced when you later considered changing employers and had to think carefully about what you were doing. The wrong decision could derail your career, and, given the family responsibilities you had assumed, it might be disastrous not just to you but to others as well. But now the risks facing you are much smaller. If the choice you make now doesn't work out, you won't have lost a great deal—primarily your time and effort—and you have the rest of your life to pursue another choice.

Assume for a moment that you have decided that you know the specific fields in which you want to be active. These fields could range from advising foreign governments to helping build your local arts festival. Now the question is, in what way will you be active? Do you see yourself as a full-time employee, as self-employed and working in your chosen field when you choose, or as a volunteer? Perhaps, if the field is new to you or if you are returning to it after an absence, your involvement will be as a student.

WORKING FOR YOURSELF

If you are comfortable with the risks, this may be just the time to become self-employed. Many financial experts point out that it's the last remaining great tax break available to Canadians, and, if you own the company, you can adopt whatever retirement age policy you like. Often a former employer is a good first client prospect. But you'll need other clients, so for this option to work well for you, you need to enjoy the prospect of marketing your services. Have you accumulated enough names on your Rolodex to make this feasible?

Self-employment is also an option for which you need to be temperamentally suited. You need to be reasonably comfortable with the inevitable uncertainties about where your next client will come from. And you should be prepared to deal with clients who pay in 60 or 90 days rather than 30 and with the inevitable ups and downs of cash flow for the self-employed. You should be used to structuring your own time and setting your own goals, because there will likely be no one but the cat to observe whether or not you are working industriously.

If you feel the downsides of self-employment will keep you awake at night, you probably will be happier as an employee, and you need to find an employer who doesn't have a mandatory retirement policy.

BUILDING A BUSINESS ON CONTACTS: DOREEN McKENZIE-SANDERS

Doreen McKenzie-Sanders has always sought out challenges. She went to study journalism as a mature, part-time student at the University of Western Ontario, and when she graduated she wanted to write about business, because "business is where the money is." The *Financial Post* hired her as a stringer.

Doreen had been working for about a year when she saw an ad seeking applicants for the position of assistant editor of a business publication. It was the *Business Quarterly,* published at Western since 1933, and the two people doing the hiring were her references! She got the job, and for the next 25 years the *Business Quarterly* (now called *Ivey Business Journal*) was home as she rose to be publisher and editor. In this job, she got to know just about everyone who wrote about business.

She also attended and eventually taught in a summer program at Harvard University on publishing procedures. She learned how to take a concept and turn it into reality, how to define the market, how to fund a publication, who would buy advertising and why—in short, everything about the business of magazine publishing.

A few years before her 100th issue of the *Quarterly,* Doreen started asking herself, "What am I going to do next?" She would have a modest pension from the university, but she knew she didn't want to stop working. She wanted to be active and feel challenged. She began setting aside money to fund her first year of business as a consultant to the publishing industry. Her plan was to work about three days a week.

As is the case for many new consultants, her first client was her former employer. The dean of the business school had received a corporate grant to commission someone to write and publish a history of the school. Who better to do the task than Doreen? She learned a great deal about the book publishing business—as distinct from magazine publishing—from that experience.

At about the same time, David S.R. Leighton, a professor at the business school, had received a large grant to do research on the role of women in business. He thought it was important to get the word out about the work being done at the university's Centre for the Study of Women in Management. Of course, he turned to Doreen for help. So, while she was writing the history of the business school she also took on the editing of the centre's *Women in Management* newsletter—a task she is still doing today, some 13 years later.

The attention that Doreen's history of the business school received when it was published led one of her former contributors to the *Quarterly* to contact her about a book he was thinking of writing. Could she help him find a publisher? Indeed, she could—by putting together a complete package that contained sample chapters, a mockup of the book, a marketing strategy and a detailed critical path from signing to publication. The publisher bought the book, Doreen earned a good fee and the author was delighted. He told his friends, and more business came along.

Like every self-employed person who lives by his or her wits, Doreen used to lie awake nights worrying whether or not she would ever get another client. She needn't have worried; her success with publishers was her best advertisement, and book development became the major part of her business. The planned three days a week turned into a full-time job, which continues to be fun and profitable. She enjoys the contact with smart people, a valuable benefit in addition to the fees she earns.

Doreen also felt she could begin contributing something to the life of her city. Long a lover of the summer music festival at Tanglewood in Western Massachusetts and a subscriber to the London Symphony Orchestra, she had a vision of bringing live music to London during the summer. In 1995, she organized the first of two summer festivals of music held in the courtyard of Huron College at the University of Western Ontario.

As Doreen looks back upon her self-employed career after the *Business Quarterly,* she delights in having had the freedom to be able to do what she wants—to work on the projects she enjoys and do as little or much as she feels like. From her student days to today, Doreen has approached life and work as a series of opportunities to learn, and she never wants to stop. In 1998, Doreen moved back to Vancouver, the city where she was born, and was pleased to escape the long winters in London.

What advice would she give to people looking forward to retirement? "Focus on the skills and talents and aspects of your current job that you most like. Then look for some opportunity to use those talents. It may take some thinking, and it may not be in anything you thought you would do, but you will know when you find it. It won't find you—you have to do a bit of looking—but, given your experience, and that is the one advantage we have on the young, you will know where to look. Regard every opportunity as a learning experience and benefit from it. Above all, enjoy what you do."

Doreen's experience provides a number of lessons.

- Life is full of opportunities to learn, and these opportunities don't disappear when you turn 60. Seize them even if it's not clear where they might lead, because they will probably lead you where you want to go.
- Starting a business requires financial and psychological preparation, but it may be a wonderful way to make full use of the learning and experience of a lifetime.
- Cultivating a wide circle of contacts in your early and middle working life may bring you unforeseen opportunities when you hang out your own shingle.

WORKING FOR WAGES

As Sylvia Ostry said, "Work is not always a disutility." Most people who have worked for a number of employers over their careers know, however, that the enjoyment and fulfillment one gets from work can vary tremendously, depending on the nature of the work and the working conditions. Even if earning money is very important, it's worth considering the intangibles that often make or break the employee's experience on the job. Are the working conditions satisfactory? Will there be constructive feedback on your performance? Will your duties and the company of your colleagues be enjoyable? Will the work meet your needs for mental stimulation and social interaction as well as your financial requirements? Now is no time to settle for a job that makes you dread Mondays.

Remember that you have a lot of knowledge and experience to offer and that an employer will be fortunate to have these assets in his or her company. So, when you interview prospective employers, don't be arrogant but also don't be submissive or self-deprecating. Your age is a positive, not a negative, factor. You have something to offer that is not easily replicated—your wisdom and experience—and employers will benefit from your services.

Of course, if you need to earn as much as possible, you may have to abandon your dream of a second career in sculpture and stay with commercial design. Perhaps you can compensate by participating in weekend or evening sculpture classes while your day job pays the rent.

PART-TIME OR CONTRACT WORK

If your preferred option is to keep on doing more or less what you have been doing, but you want to change your job description to include more tasks you like—or you simply want to reduce your work week—spend some time thinking about what that means to you and to the company. It may mean your job is redefined as part-time rather than full-time or that you cease being an employee and become an independent contractor.

There are some real advantages to the company in working with you to arrive at a mutually satisfactory arrangement. It is, after all, retaining someone who is familiar with how it operates, its clients or customers and its products or services; you have detailed and firm-specific knowledge that only comes with the passage of time. At the same time, if you are cutting back, someone will have to pick up the slack, and that may require some juggling of the workforce. Your objective should be to obtain the conditions of work you desire without being exploited. The deal you strike should be beneficial to both parties, or it will not endure very long.

You need to ask what your new work arrangements will mean to your pensions, your tax status and your package of benefits. If the company is no longer making contributions for your benefits and pension, would it consider covering the full cost of the maximum deduction for an RRSP? Get some professional advice on these matters; over a period of five or more years the financial implications could be quite significant to you and your dependants.

VOLUNTEERING

If you don't have to worry about earning income but endless leisure is not appealing, you may want to volunteer your services in a worthy cause. Doing your research is even more important here, if you're going to be working entirely for intangible rewards, than if you're working for money. If your valuable services are free to the organization of your choice, there may not be strong enough economic incentives for it to use your time and talents efficiently and effectively. And the last thing you want to do is waste time and effort when you could be accomplishing something important elsewhere.

Consider interviewing the organization that you might be volunteering to help. Not all not-for-profit groups are the same; some know how to use volunteers effectively, but others are so wrapped up in their worthy mission that they give little time or thought to developing volunteer workers and to determining how to use them for maximum mutual benefit.

It's very useful to have a contact within the organization who can give you a preview of what is involved in volunteering there. Ask for the names of some of the other volunteers who work for the organization, and interview them. Get their opinions, not on the worthiness of the organization and its goals (these should be self-evident), but on whether or not it is well run. Here are some questions to ask.

1. Is the turnover of volunteer staff low or high, and why?
2. Is there a designated volunteer coordinator, and what are that person's qualifications?
3. Are there job descriptions for volunteers, and does the organization provide regular feedback on performance?
4. Is there a mechanism to provide for backup when you are out of town, ill or otherwise unavailable?

5. Is there a forum for volunteers to make proposals to management for improvements in the use of volunteers?

Remember to compare a volunteer opportunity with other options, just as you would compare two competing job offers. Since you have done the thinking about your strengths and preferences, you know what you are offering and you know what you need in return. If there is doubt in your mind after your research, put the option to one side and look at others before trying to convince yourself that in spite of your doubts "things will work out." Your volunteer commitment should be enjoyable and not stress-building. If it is not rewarding to you and to the organization, you should change your plan—no matter how worthy the cause.

GOING BACK TO SCHOOL

An increasingly popular option for the recently retired is going back to school, sometimes for practical training but more often just for the excitement of learning. If this appeals to you, talk to someone at the institution you're considering about what programs they offer, especially for senior students. Try to interview one or two senior students to find out if they had any problems or concerns, how interesting or useful they found the course of study and how they fit into the campus routine.

Ask yourself: If I am going back to school, what do I expect and how realistic is it? Does the school have other senior students? Will I fit in? Can I make a contribution that will benefit both me and the institution?

EXAMPLES FROM REAL LIFE

Life is not a dress rehearsal. Whatever your choices—and there are as many paths to fulfillment as there are individuals to follow them—try above all to avoid the empty disappointment expressed in the popular song made famous by Peggy Lee: "Is that all there is?"

Think back to the people you have met in these pages and the creative ways in which they fashioned their varying "retirements." For Peter Lougheed, maximizing income was not the dominant consideration, because he had a pension from his years in government and was prepared to budget within it. He wanted to stay in the West, in his home base of Calgary, where he had an extensive circle of friends and where he felt comfortable. Political life had taken its toll in countless rubber-chicken events that required many nights away from home, and he wanted to enjoy a slower pace. Nevertheless, he looked forward to travel for both business and pleasure.

Margaret Labarge wanted to stay put as well, but she knew that for most of her research she would have to visit the great libraries in North America and Europe. Although she liked travelling, she wanted a home base where she had friends and where she could be a part of the community.

For Alcid and George Yelle, while some supplement to pension income was welcome, the chief priority was to keep active doing the things they liked. Alcid did beekeeping and woodworking and now Parkinson's Society work, and George and his wife run the fishing camp and guide tourists. They enjoy being active, and they want to do things that give them pleasure.

Gordon Watson had an adequate pension, which allowed him to indulge his love of archaeology. While Shaun Butler could attain his "dream retirement" of living in beautiful Cape Cod and playing golf, he found "all leisure, all the time" was not for him and quickly arrived at a more rewarding balance of work and leisure.

Perhaps this is a good time to tell the story—so far—of David's "retirement." After a varied career in which he held many jobs (none of them for very long, as his official bio says) in academia, government and banking, David retired—for the first time, at least—in 1998, at the age of 60, because his employer had a policy of mandatory retirement at 60. A number of his slightly younger colleagues, unhappy with the prospect of mandatory retirement themselves, suggested he mount a legal challenge. David knew such a challenge might quite likely succeed and judged that the risk he might find himself working full time for five more years was too great. He decided to go quietly. And, in truth, since he had been gleefully posting the number of days until his "forced" retirement daily almost since he joined the bank at age 50, his credibility as a crusader for older employees' rights might have been a little suspect.

But, like the duck who glides along the surface of the pond, all the while paddling furiously but invisibly below the water, the enthusiastic would-be retiree was laying the groundwork for life after 60. He knew he would like to return to teaching at the university level post-bank-retirement; as he is fond of saying, "Teaching is the only form of show business I know that has a guaranteed income." He approached the Faculty of Commerce at the University of British Columbia, offering to teach some courses each year as an adjunct professor. Since he had been an assistant professor many years previously as a newly minted Ph.D. and since teaching introductory finance is not the most coveted teaching assignment for full-time faculty, he was taken on at once. As his retirement date neared, he approached the dean about a full-time teaching schedule (but definitely not including the committee work and other administrative duties normally expected of a full time faculty member); since his course evaluations were good, the dean signed him up for four years.

During his last several years of full-time employment with the bank, David had written a weekly column on an economic topic of general interest as well as a more in-depth quarterly bulletin on a topic of current interest. Turning out over 400 weekly articles had certainly sharpened his writing skills—and it was a task he enjoyed. About six months before the planned retirement date, he proposed an arrangement with his employer to continue after retirement as a consultant, writing his weekly newsletter, providing interest rate forecasts, drafting speeches for bank executives and speaking to clients. The bank, showing a fine appreciation of the weak underpinnings of its mandatory retirement policy—and possibly also relieved that it wouldn't have to hire another economist when David retired—agreed. What David did not keep were the administrative burdens of his old job.

In the course of fulfilling his public affairs responsibilities with the bank, David had also been doing a lot of public speaking, for bank clients and also for local business and community service organizations. Since the weekly newsletter he wrote on economic issues for the bank's clients was also carried in the local newspaper, and since he often commented about economic news on radio and TV, he began to be quite well-known. Upon retirement, David was free to sign up with an agent and could accept speaking engagements as a self-employed person.

For David, this "portfolio" approach worked well. He had an office at the university and access to the U.B.C. libraries, he enjoyed the stimulation of discourse with a group of highly intelligent fellow faculty members and, most importantly, he had the opportunity to interact with students—something he had always enjoyed. In his various speaking "gigs" he could capitalize on his love of performing. The day after his retirement party, David, a little the worse for wear, flew off to an out-of-town speaking engagement. The week after his "retirement," he was complaining about the 12-hour workdays in his newly outfitted home office and at the university. In fact, he still complains, but admits that he enjoys everything he does. He also has a luxury not always available to employees: he can turn down work he doesn't want to take on.

He delighted in having more free time to pursue other interests such as writing this book and tackling a reading list that seemed to get longer rather than shorter. He became much more proficient in making bread—something in which he took special pleasure. While he still looked forward to a move out of the

Lower Mainland, he was also mindful that Diane was running a business and was not in a position to move for several years.

DECIDING WHERE YOU WANT TO LIVE

Some of the most successful moves seem to be those where the new arrivals are returning to a place where they lived happily at an earlier time in their lives. We have friends who retired to their college town in New Hampshire to take advantage of all the interesting university activities they could share in as alumni. Though they had lived for many years in a warmer climate, they cheerfully bought a light truck and don't seem to mind the snow. Another couple who had lived in many cities in Canada and abroad during the husband's career with a financial institution returned to settle in Vancouver—the scene of an earlier career posting. They found that making their way into the social and cultural life of the city was a real challenge, but they are now happy with their choice.

Perhaps the most important thing that needs to be said about making the choice to move is that it should not be made quickly. Get to know the place you are considering very well—*before* you bid on that desirable property. Perhaps you can schedule vacations there; try to visit over several years and at different times of the year. Perhaps your friends know people who have lived there and can put you in touch with them. Collect literature on your proposed new town or city, or subscribe to the local newspaper and read all about your prospective community every week for a year.

Most important of all, don't put a "For Sale" sign on your

present home—especially if you are ambivalent about moving—until you find a place you truly prefer. It's delightful to make a killing in the real estate market, but you don't want to find yourself in receipt of an offer you can't refuse without having a place to go that you can look forward to with excitement and enthusiasm.

In our case, we were both interested in moving out of the Lower Mainland to escape traffic gridlock and incessant rain and, since our families and friends are scattered all across the continent, our main concern was to chose a place where they would want to visit us. While we aspire to country quiet, we are not at all talented at wilderness living or driving long distances. We are not really interested in the availability of professional sports but believe that a good wine store and a well-stocked and diverse grocery store are essential.

In 1999, after a year of research, we purchased an investment/retirement property about an hour's drive outside Calgary, near Banff, where we had frequently vacationed. It combined access to cultural facilities and good bookstores with a quieter lifestyle and great scenic beauty. It was also easily accessible to Calgary's increasingly sophisticated urban centre, the Trans-Canada Highway and an international airport. For two more years, we spent as much time as possible "trying out" our prospective home in all seasons. We told ourselves that, if we eventually concluded that a decision to live there full time did not seem right, the place would, in any case, be a good investment. We finally made the move in late 2001, at a point when relocation made sense for us both—though we argued about the date a lot. The process was a powerful reminder that moving house is always a major upheaval, even if you have come to the decision only very slowly and with careful deliberation.

Nevertheless, we've been very happy with our decision. It has meant returning to long and often bitterly cold winters, but it also means bright skies all year long. Our families and friends find it an attractive and accessible place to visit. Our business interests are such that, with a high-speed Internet connection and proximity to Calgary International Airport, we can manage our various commitments with a little planning. Thus we could make our personal interest in arts and culture a dominant factor in our choice.

EVALUATING AND REVISITING

There's no doubt that the benefits of a step-by-step planning process are almost immeasurable—even if the result is a plan that doesn't involve earning any money at all. The people profiled in this book all found ways to adapt positively to changes in their working lives. Often they jettisoned responsibilities they disliked or had grown tired of, and they progressed to another set in which they found an active, challenging and diverse range of activities that gave them immense pleasure and contentment. These fruits of your labour, not money, are the best rewards.

Circumstances will certainly change, and your interests and priorities may also change. From time to time, do a reality check and make adjustments to your plan. Recognize the benefits of always looking forward, even as you enjoy reminiscence of good times past.

Conclusion

Putting It All Together

It's time for a quick review before you launch on your voyage of fulfillment and discovery.

First, remember that the years after 60 or 65 really do have the potential to be golden. You have the benefit of a lifetime of experience and wisdom and, if you use those assets for your own benefit, you will be able to create a truly rewarding life. No one will be telling you what to do and when to do it. If you have the blessing of good health, the main constraints facing you will be the ones that you yourself will set. Under such conditions, your life after full-time work will be rich in enjoyment and fulfillment—if you take the time and make the effort to prepare now. Like the long-anticipated return on an investment made patiently over many years, your retirement years can be the dividend on a lifetime of learning those lessons that only time can teach.

The most important message of this book is that creating a plan for the rest of your life is one of the best investments you can make. This plan concerns what you want to do and how you want to live; it is not a financial plan. Think of it as creating a road map for the future, whereas your financial plan will provide the gas for the car. Like a road map, your life plan will not tell you which road to take at every turn in order to reach your goal, but it will give you tremendous help in making those decisions when you come to them. A plan will allow you to recognize opportunities and capitalize on them, and perhaps even help you find a way to turn adversity into opportunity. It will give you guidelines against which to measure the psychic return you achieve from the investment of your time in the various activities you choose. Most importantly, it will put you in touch with yourself.

Developing a plan requires thought, honesty with yourself and trust in those who know you best. You have to think about what it is that you like and dislike. Then you must be honest with yourself in evaluating your strengths and weaknesses. This process of doing an inventory of you and your abilities is not an easy task. It is hard work and perhaps a bit terrifying, but the rewards you will gain from doing it with care and thoroughness cannot be overemphasized. The prime beneficiary of that care and completeness is you, so why would you want to cheat yourself? Finally, you have to trust your friends and your significant other to give you honest feedback on what you believe those strengths and weaknesses are.

When you have done this spadework, it's on to the exciting business of researching and evaluating opportunities—whether these are opportunities to work for others, to work for yourself or to volunteer your time in a cause you find compelling. They may flow from your career experience, from personal contacts or from a boyhood or girlhood enthusiasm that you finally have time to pursue.

Not only will you want to consider what you want to do, but also where you want to do it. If your circumstances give you a great deal of choice in this matter, it is extremely important to research your options and make your plans with care—and with the full participation of those closest to you.

Of course, you can survive without a plan, and if you are lucky and resilient—as is our fishmonger, Ken Fiddes—you may do much better than survive. But what we have been discussing in this book is not surviving but flourishing, enjoying life to the maximum, making every minute count by contributing to your own and others' welfare. If there is one theme unifying the stories of the men and women we talked to in preparing this book, it is their passionate involvement in what they are doing right now, rather than in past triumphs or tragedies. The past is to learn from; the present is to live.

Gordon Watson at the age of 85 is embarked on the excavation of a new archaeological site that by his own estimate will take 30 years to complete. Tom McCabe is delighted with his "second career" in theatre management and has no plan to retire anytime soon. Joy Coghill is deep into the effort to raise funding for a home for retired actors. Paddy Sherman is still clambering up mountains and teaching his grandson the joys of climbing. Each of the people portrayed in this book has found his or her own way to continue enjoying life through endeavours that are meaningful to them. Their joy is in doing, not merely in being. Surviving is not in their lexicon—living life to the fullest is their guiding principle.

Another key message of this book is that preparation for this period of your life is not something that can be done in a day or a week. It takes more than 20 years of training for most young people to enter into the adult world of work. The time after full-time work will probably last just as long as your career and requires more preparation than an afternoon's reflection. Just reviewing all the Web sites included in Appendix B will take a couple of days. So start thinking about the future well before you leave the world of full-time work behind. Give yourself time to research and think through all your options and their ramifications. Make sure that the plan you embark upon makes sense for you and those nearest you.

And remember, any good plan allows for change. As you age, you may have to give up some activities and trade them for others. Peter Lougheed might have been forced to relinquish some directorships of public companies because of age, but he still is contributing enthusiastically and effectively to debates on public policy.

Adjusting to changing conditions is nothing new; we have all had to do it throughout our lives. But having the wisdom to accept change and to identify the goals and opportunities that still remain within your reach will enable you to live life to the fullest, even if circumstances change in unforeseen ways. In spite of seemingly overwhelming adversity, Alcide Yelle turned his affliction with Parkinson's into an opportunity to use his talents for organization to help in fighting the disease. He takes justifiable pride in his work; in listening to him, you catch his conviction that a cure can be found and you catch his excitement when the annual walk for Parkinson's is held in the nation's capital.

Finally, ask yourself what you want to look back on if you are fortunate enough to reach a great age, as our friend Tom Brown has. His is the perfect example to illustrate all that we have been saying in this book.

A GOOD INNINGS: TOM BROWN

Tom Brown is a genuine Second World War hero who, in his 90s, is slowing down a bit. But he still loves to fly-fish, reads insatiably and is as quick with a comment as ever. A Rhodes Scholar from the University of British Columbia, he studied jurisprudence at Oxford University. Returning to Vancouver in 1936, he had a short career in stock brokering before going off to war. Wounded on the beaches of Normandy, he was awarded the MBE for bravery. When he was demobilized, he went into business with his father providing investment advice for clients in Vancouver

From the start, the employees of Odlum Brown owned the company, and the shares were traded strictly at book value—meaning they increased in value only if some part of the profits were retained in the firm. Tom wanted to ensure that the younger members of the firm not feel that the "old fogies," as he referred to himself, would hang around forever. He wanted to ensure the continual renewal of the firm. In

1966, close to his 54th birthday, he put in place a policy that would require every employee to sell 20 per cent of his or her shares, beginning at age 65, for each of the next five years. Five years, Tom reasoned, would give a person enough time to phase into retirement.

This plan for a phased shift of control in the firm marked the beginning of his personal retirement planning. As Tom saw it, he would take off more and more time and eventually he would be doing no work. He and his wife, Daphne, planned their changing lifestyle with care.

Even in his 50s, Tom was not just planning, he was testing things out. Dedicated as he was to the company, he gave a lot of time to his family and volunteer commitments. Apart from gardening, about which both he and his wife Daphne were passionate, his "off-work" hours were filled with reading, travelling and volunteer service in everything from the Boy Scouts to the Anglican Theological College's board.

Tom knew instinctively that he would have to find ways to remain intellectually engaged once he left the firm entirely at 70. He had seen many of his contemporaries just give up and wait to die, and he wanted to avoid such a fate. He planned to continue handling the financial affairs of a few clients. He would maintain his contacts with the business community through serving on corporate and not-for-profit boards and a weekly luncheon club.

Tom's personal life suddenly fell apart when Daphne was diagnosed with terminal cancer. For Tom, who was still two years short of a final break with his firm when Daphne died, his continued involvement with the affairs of the company proved a godsend in helping him to cope with his loss. But now he was not just changing his daily routine as work put fewer demands on his time. He was also adjusting to a new single life and a new dwelling. Any one of these factors involves a lot of stress. Yet Tom came out of this sad period prepared to move on.

By age 70, he had turned over most of his clients to other officers of the firm. He kept only a few personal friends and continued to act as an executor for the estates of friends. He was still actively involved in not-for-profit boards. He travelled more, devoted more time to his grandchildren and great-grandchildren and played bridge at least once a week.

Tom resigned from his executor position of one final estate in 1997, at the age of 85. He just thought he was not current enough in the market to do an adequate job and, as he said, "It was no longer fun."

The loss of most of his eyesight means that his reading is now in the form of talking books. His mind, however, is still lively, he still enjoys the symphony, he continues as an active member of his luncheon club, and he is a delightful companion for lunch or dinner. Not incidentally, the firm he built continues to flourish under the direction of the person he recruited.

Looking back, he views his retirement as being a continuum from 65 to 85; he just gradually moved from full employment to none. He believes he has had a successful retirement. The ingredients of this success have been financial independence, a willingness to take advantage of opportunities as they appear, keeping active mentally, enjoying each day and filling it with interesting people and a variety of activities. As Tom said, "The needs, desires and activities change. You go from one phase of your life into another, but be ready to respond in a positive fashion to opportunities that are presented to you."

Tom's planning for the years after 65 highlights a number of important lessons.

- If you are an owner/manager of a business, take measures early to signal your intentions to those who will be in charge later. In other words, being in control and being able to set your own retirement timetable does not mean that you can get along without a timetable. Tom neatly avoided being one of those owner/managers who is eventually carried out—or forced out.
- Develop in your 40s and 50s those leisure or volunteer interests you think will bring you satisfaction in later years. If all you do is work, when work is over, what will you do?
- Recognize that, if the intellectual challenges or human associations you find through your work are important to you, you will need to make specific plans to perpetuate these in some way. If you suffer a personal loss or physical

disability in later life, active work or volunteer commitments may be the key to maintaining interest and involvement in life.

- Finally, imagine yourself as a senior. If you are fortunate, like Tom, to reach a ripe age, what do you want to be able to look back on?

Notes

CHAPTER 1

1. See Harvey Schachter, "Forget the Suit, Get Me an Anvil: A Growing Number of Executive Renegades Are Finding Satisfaction and Profits in Unconventional Careers," *Canadian Business,* vol. 70, no. 4 (April 1997), pp. 68–72.
2. One book that seems to be based solely upon this idea is Jeremy Rifkin's *The End of Work: The Decline of the Global Labor Force and the Dawn of the Post Market Era* (New York: Putnam, 1996). It would appear that he has looked at little demographic data for North America.
3. The smart personnel people are already thinking about retaining rather than firing older workers. See Douglas H. Powell, "Aging Baby Boomers: Stretching Your Workforce Options," *HR Magazine,* vol. 43, no. 8 (July 1998), pp. 82–85, and his other article, "Retaining Third-seasoners: The Time is Ripe," *Healthcare Executive,* vol. 14, no. 6 (November/December 1999), pp. 6–10. Also see Michele Himmelberg, "Aging Workforce Spells Crises: As There Will Be Fewer Young Workers, Older Workers Will Be in Demand," *Edmonton Journal,* March 13, 1999, p. I1.

4. See P.J. Wade, "Yes You Can Teach an Old Dog New Tricks," *Financial Post,* November 24, 1999, p. E2. The professional literature for gerontology in particular is full of articles illustrating the learning abilities of people well into their 70s. A nice piece is Paul Fuller, "Starting Over in Elliot Lake: Retirement Community's Institute for Learning in Retirement," *Highgrader Magazine: A Voice of the Northland,* vol. 5, no. 2 (March/April 1999), p. 30.
5. Increasingly, seniors are working past age 65 because they like working. See Tyrone Beason, "Retirees Do It for Love or Money: It May Be a Four Letter Word, but Many Seniors Are Heading Back to Full or Part-time Work," *Financial Post,* November 24, 1999, p. C16. Others are finding they have no choice. See Michael Kane, "Work Starting to Cut into Retirement, Study Shows: Unable to Support Themselves Financially, Many People Find Staying at Work Is Becoming Essential," *Vancouver Sun,* October 28, 1998, p. D1.
6. Their recent in-depth publication on the subject is *A Portrait of Seniors in Canada,* 3rd ed. (1999), cat. no. 89-519-XPE.
7. You are never too old to work, if you want to. See Charles Laurence, "It Was Depressing When I Retired: On this Bonne Bell Production Line the Average Age is 70. Is This the 'Senior Center' of the Future?" *National Post,* April 3, 2001.

CHAPTER 2

1. William Shakespeare, *As You Like It,* Act II, Scene vii.
2. Kevin Milligan, Quebec's *Baby Bonus: Can Public Policy Raise Fertility?* Toronto: C.D. Howe Institute, January 24, 2002.
3. David Baxter, Jim Smerdon and Andrew Ramlo, *Forty Million: Canada's Population in the Next Four Decades* (Vancouver: Urban Futures Institute, June 1999).

CHAPTER 3

1. A great deal of statistical information exists on Canadian women of all ages. One of the easiest places to begin searching is with Statistics Canada. We recommend going to the Web site of *The Daily* (www.statcan.ca/english/dai-quo/). By using the search facility on that page, you can locate all the basic Statistics Canada publications and data sources, and they are numerous. Much of the information is available in electronic form for easy downloading. One source we recommend is *Women in Canada: Work Chapter Updates,* cat. no. 89FO133XIE, an annual publication. Two other publications provide useful context: *Eldercare in Canada: Context, Content and Consequences* (November 1999), cat. no. 89-570-XPE, and *A Portrait of Seniors in Canada,* 3rd ed. (1999), cat. no. 89-519-XPE. Most university libraries and major public libraries have copies of these documents; Statistics Canada offices across Canada also have a library open to the public.
2. According to Statistics Canada, in a recent *Perspectives on Labour and Income,* cat. no. 75-001-XIE (based on the *1997 Survey of Labour Income and Dynamics*), average annual earnings for Canadian women were only 61.6 per cent of those for men. Women's hourly wages, however, were 80.4 per cent of men's. Thus, on average, women work fewer hours than men do and receive lower compensation for their time at work.
3. Again, according to Statistics Canada, low income for a single person varies according to location. For example, in 2000 a single person with a low income and living in rural area would have an after-tax income of $9,947 or less, while the cut-off would rise to $15,172 for a person living in an urban centre with a population of over 500,000. There figures are taken from yet another Statistics Canada publication, *Low Income Cutoffs*

from 1991 to 2000 and Low Income Measures from 1990 to 1999, cat. no. 75F0002MIE2001007.

CHAPTER 4

1. See C.T. Gillin and Thomas R. Klassen, "Retire Mandatory Retirement," *Policy Options Politiques,* July–August 2000. This article is an excellent and succinct discussion, from the point of view of two sociologists, of the pernicious effect of outmoded mandatory retirement laws.
2. *McKinney v. Board of Governors of the University of Guelph et al.,* 63 Ontario Reports (2d) 1, 46 D.L.R. (4th) 193, 37 C.R.R. 44 (Ont.C.A.).
3. Donald C. Dunlop, *Mandatory Retirement: A Human Rights Decision?* (Toronto: Conference Board of Canada, January 1980). A major Canadian research organization estimated more than 20 years ago that in any one year, 0.1 per cent of the labour force, at most, would *choose to* continue working past the age of 65 and that this would have little impact on national output, pension costs or the need for income support programs. Nothing more recent can be found in the literature.
4. Relaxing any or all of these conditions will not change the basic facts, but sorting out the impact of different assumptions can get terribly confusing.
5. "Present value" refers to the value to you today of cash you expect to receive in future. Clearly, $10,000 next year is less valuable to you than $10,000 now—by at least the amount of interest you could earn on the $10,000 if you had it right now. This rate of interest is your discount rate—the rate by which you discount future cash to determine what the right to receive a future payment is worth to you now. Thus, the analytical method is called "discounted cash-flow analysis."

Appendix A

Personal Planning Worksheets

EXERCISE 1—WRITING YOUR AUTOBIOGRAPHY

The objective is to recall the events or experiences in your life which were most important to you. Remember to include both accomplishments and difficulties. You might begin by doing a rough, point-form draft of the highlights and low points of various periods of your life. You can use the following headings—or as many as apply to you:

A. *Growing up*

___

___

___

B. *School through graduation from high school*

___

___

___

C. *Further education or professional training*

D. *My first job*

E. *Life in my 20s*

F. *Big events between 30 and 50*

G. *Big events since I turned 50.*

Leave yourself room for filling in points that you might have missed. Then, put your draft aside and come back to it after three or four days. Did you skip something? Remember that this is for your eyes only, so be honest with yourself and don't gloss over something that was unpleasant or stressful or that you might not have handled in the best way. Each major experience in our lives shapes us and tells us something about ourselves, and that is what you hope to discover as you write your biography.

Now, allocate some quiet time for the detailed work. For each event in each period make a separate page, with headings something like those shown below. Now look at each event or experience that you thought was important enough to put into your life story. Why was it important? How did you or do you feel about it; was it a happy or a sad time; does something about it give you pleasure or pain in recollection? Would you want to repeat it? Why? And finally, how do you feel this event or experience shaped your life? Some advice: Take your time.

Event/experience:

____

Year/decade:

____

Why is it important?

____

How did I feel about it?

____

Would I do it again?

____

Main lesson or skill learned?

____

EXERCISE 2—IDENTIFYING LIKES AND DISLIKES, STRENGTHS AND WEAKNESSES

Once you have done the biography exercise and believe you have made an honest and complete summary of the important events or experiences, read over your work and ask yourself the following questions. Write down the answers in the following spaces, or provide your own list of answers.

A. What are the things you really like and do not like doing? (A list of four to six should be adequate.)

____

____

____

____

____

____

B. Then rank the activities or situations in A. Which of these activities do you like most and dislike most? (Rank them.) Do any of them depend on living in a particular place? (If so, write that down.)

Likes *Location*

____

____

____

____

____

____

Dislikes *Location*

C. *Finally, after reading over your autobiographical notes, what would you consider,* on the basis of what you have written, *to be your greatest strengths and biggest weaknesses? Rank them, and be able to explain why they are on the list and what accounts for their ranking.*

Strengths, in order *Reason*

Weaknesses, in order (just a few!) *Reason*

D. *Don't forget to validate your list with three or four friends or associates who will be as honest with you as you have been with yourself!*

Persons to be approached for validation

Alternates

EXERCISE 3—MAKING CHOICES AND SETTING GOALS

The third step is an exercise in triangulation—a fancy term for finding how to use your strengths and likes and location preferences to find what is best for you.

For example, David identified his abilities as a teacher and a public speaker and his love of an audience. In his preparation for retirement from his job with the bank, he concentrated on finding opportunities to do both—leading to university teaching and professional public speaking after leaving his job at the bank. He also identified strength in writing and a love of history, which has led to writing a history of banking in Canada. His enthusiasm for libraries led to his volunteer work for the library at the Banff Centre.

Now, you have a try at setting your goals. It may be helpful to write down why you believe each goal or activity will give you personal satisfaction.

Long-term Goals/Projects

A.

Because:

B.

Because:

C.

Because:

Short-term Goals/Projects (optional)

A.

____

Because:

____

B.

____

Because:

____

C.

____

Because:

____

You may want to use the Web site listings in Appendix B to start you on the road to finding opportunities where you can use your talents to their best advantage. Use Appendix B and the links on many of the Web pages, and you should have a sizable portfolio of information that you can narrow down until you find perhaps four primary targets. Then do research on each target and think about how you might begin to approach each one. Remember, this is not something to begin doing a month before retirement. Give yourself plenty of time, and do it well. An investment of time and effort today means a long period of productive and fulfilling activity thereafter.

Good luck!

Appendix B

Internet Sources for Retirement Planning

There are three general or comprehensive Web sites with which you may want to begin your research. Each one has a host of different links to other Web sites. They are:

www.2young2retire.com—A site published by Howard and Marika Stone for those 50 and over who are looking for information on retirement.

www.50plus.com—This is the site of the Canadian Association of Retired People, now known as Canada's Association for the Fifty-Plus.

www.aarp.org—This is the site of the American Association of Retired Persons, now known by its acronym, AARP.

The list below includes approximately 100 Web sites on a wide range of general and specialized topics; it is current as of September 2002. However, new sites are being added all the time. Check the three listed above for the latest additions or use a search engine such as Google; just put in some key words and see what you find. And of course your reference librarian at your local public library will be willing to help you find your way through the Internet thicket. Please note that we have not included sites focused narrowly on financial planning.

In some cases in the following list, we have indicated the geographical scope of the site-whether it is international or limited to just the U.S.A. or Canada. In other cases, the title of the Web site or the notes make the scope or coverage of the site clear, or geographical scope is not relevant (as with many health sites).

If anything, there is almost too much information available on the Web. With a little practice, however, you will soon learn how to phrase your searches so they retrieve just the wheat and not the chaff. Good luck in finding the information you need!

1. VOLUNTEER LINKS

Actions Without Borders (http://www.idealist.org/)
Scope: International
Idealist, a project initiated by Actions Without Borders, is the most comprehensive directory of non-profit and volunteering resources on the Web. The site includes links to 22,000 non-profit and community organizations, volunteer centres and museums in 150 countries. Volunteer opportunities, non-profit jobs and internships, services and resources are listed. The site also features search engines that facilitate accessing information by country, organization, type of work sought, and so on.

Canadian Executive Service Organization (CESO) (http://www.ceso-saco.com)
Scope: Canada
CESO is a not-for-profit organization that recruits qualified volunteer advisers to work with Aboriginal peoples of Canada, and with the peoples of developing nations and emerging market economies, to promote economic and social growth.

Canyonlands Field Institute (CFI) (http://www.canyonlandsfieldinst.org/)
Scope: U.S.A. and international
The site promotes the courses and activities carried out by the Institute. Courses for students of all ages are included. Most importantly, CFI is also academic host for "Elderhostel," a non-profit international organization offering educational adventures for older adults looking for new challenges and expanded horizons. CFI programs are targeted to active elders and their spouses of any age.

Coaching and Mentoring Children (http://216.66.7.60)
Scope: Based in the U.S.A., it has expanded into Canada, Australia and the United Kingdom
This is the site of Future Possibilities, a non-profit organization involved in providing coaching for children ages 7 to 12. Volunteers are first trained to become "Kid-coaches."

Cross-Cultural Solutions (http://www.volunteerworkabroad.org)
Scope: U.S.A-based—international
Cross-Cultural Solutions is an independent, non-religious, non-profit organization employing volunteer humanitarian action to empower communities, foster cultural understanding, and identify grassroots solutions to global challenges. The organization works in partnership with more than 100 non-profit humanitarian organizations around the world, including both large, international NGOs and grassroots organizations. Volunteer programs are displayed on the site.

Environmental Alliance for Senior Involvement (http://www.easi.org)
Scope: International
The site lists volunteer opportunities and jobs as volunteer coordinators. The site also has bulletin boards with public and volunteer forums that provide users with opportunities to exchange opinions and to expand their contacts with persons interested in environmental issues and activities.

Experience Corps® (http://www.experiencecorps.org/)
Scope: U.S.A.
Experience Corps® provides schools and youth organizations with help from caring older adults to improve academic performance, to make schools more caring places, and to strengthen ties between schools and youth organizations and their neighbourhoods, while also enhancing the well-being of volunteers.

411 Seniors Centre (http://www.411seniors.bc.ca)
Scope: Canada (British Columbia)
The 411 Seniors Centre is an easily accessible social and recreational drop-in facility for seniors. The site provides information concerning the centre's programs: social and volunteer activities, multicultural programs, future projects.

Habitat for Humanity International (http://www.habitat.org/)
Scope: International
Habitat for Humanity International is a non-profit, non-denominational Christian organization. Its purpose is to build simple, affordable housing in partnership with those in need of adequate shelter. Habitat for Humanity International has more than 1,700 affiliates in more than 55 countries around the world. In Canada, there are 49 affiliates that can be contacted locally. The site offers links to volunteer and salaried positions.

The Hunger Site (http://www.thehungersite.com/cgi-bin/WebObjects/CTDSites)
Scope: International
Focused on donations—the self description is "click-to-donate site." Donations are received from throughout the world. Funds are used to help hungry people in more than 74 countries.

International Work Camps (http://www.vfp.org/)
Scope: International
The site contains information on volunteering throughout the world (including Canada). Volunteering opportunities are searchable by country, dates and type of camp (includes an "elder" section). There is a rich "Links" page that includes Web sites of a number of organizations and volunteering opportunities. Volunteer for Peace, the organization sponsoring the Web site, also has an annual newsletter available upon request and free of charge.

National Retiree Volunteer Coalition (http://www.nrvc.org/)
Scope: U.S.A. and Canada (Alberta)
The coalition initiates programs and partnerships to facilitate retirees helping communities in various areas: mentoring, library development, expanding computer programs, etc. The idea is to transform the expertise of retirees into community leadership and service. There are also links to other U.S. volunteer organizations.

The Nature Conservancy (http://nature.org/)
Scope: U.S.A. and international
Applications for membership are received from all over the world. The site offers publications, legal information and ongoing activities. There is a Canada Program as well.

Oxfam International (http://www.oxfam.org/)
Scope: International (there is an Oxfam office in Canada)
Oxfam International (OI) is a growing confederation of autonomous non-governmental organizations, committed to working together to fight poverty and injustice around the world.

Save the Children (http://www.savethechildren.org)
Scope: U.S.A. and international
Although it is based in the U.S.A., the organization receives applications from all over the world. The focus is to help children who suffer due to famine, lack of shelter, disasters after wars or natural hazards, etc. The site highlights current issues and has a link to Publications. The site enables various ways of helping: donations, sponsorship or volunteering.

Sierra Club (http://www.sierraclub.org)
Scope: U.S.A. and international; Canadians may apply to become members at http://www.sierraclub.ca
Sierra Club is a U.S. environmental organization that now has more than 700,000 members. The site offers three search engines: one enables searches by the issue of interest, another accesses the latest events, issues and chapters by geographical area, and a third searches through Sierra Club's publications over the years by topic/keyword.

Volunteer Grandparents (http://mypage.direct.ca/v/vgps/school.html)
Scope: Canada
The Volunteer Grandparents Society of Canada is a non-profit organization that has been operating for 26 years. The Society has developed a school-based grandparenting program with the goal of matching seniors to school classes so they can provide a support for children.

Volunteer Vancouver (http://www.vancouver.volunteer.ca)
Scope: Canada (British Columbia)
The site reflects volunteer opportunities in Vancouver and Greater Vancouver. There is a search engine for volunteer positions organized on the site by broad areas of interest, by preferred work location and by age groups (age 50+ included). Volunteer Vancouver also has a library; the catalogue is available on the Internet but only members can borrow.

West Edmonton Seniors (http://www.ecn.ab.ca/westsen/index.html)
Scope: Canada (Alberta)
The mission of this centre is to provide wellness programs and other services to members and non-members in Edmonton and the surrounding area. Programs are targeted to improve quality of life in later years by encouraging individuals to remain physically active and involved.

2. BUSINESS AND CAREER LINKS

Canada.com (http://www.canada.com/national)
Scope: Canada
Canada.com is a comprehensive Internet network and portal operated by CanWest Interactive. More than 30 Southam publications and other online newspapers, carclick.com and careerclick.com support the canada.com network by supplying up-to-date news and information. Canada.com is also a full-service portal for personalized information and services including travel, autos, careers, finance, free e-mail, news, shopping, sports, and a business and people directory.

The Caretaker Gazette (http://www.caretaker.org)
Scope: U.S.A. and international
The Caretaker Gazette is a newsletter containing property caretaking and house-sitting opportunities, advice and information for property caretakers, house-sitters and landowners. Each issue has 130 or more caretaking and house-sitting positions throughout the U.S.A. and overseas.

Entrepreneur Magazine (http://www.entrepreneurmag.com)
This is a useful site in terms of providing an array of information on how to establish and manage a business. It is interactive and has good resources.

Franchise Links (http://www.franchisecentral.com)
On this site one can learn what franchising is and how it works for many individuals and organizations throughout the world.

Midlife Mentor (http://www.midlifementor.com)
The site addresses women going through mid-life changes. Solutions such as coaching and mentoring are suggested; tele-classes and teleconferences offer an interactive approach. Resources and useful links are also available.

Senior Job Bank Canada (http://www.seniorjobbank.org/Canada)
Scope: Canada
This is a non-profit referral service. Jobs, résumés and skills can be posted. The site has a search engine to help users locate the desired information.

Solo Self-employment (Working Solo) (http://www.workingsolo.com)
The site offers information on topics such as how to start a business in general and how to build an e-business; it also provides links to resources.

Work/Life Based on Values (Resources For Success)
(http://www.philiphumbert.com)
This site was set up by Dr. Philip E. Humbert, Ph.D., an author, speaker and professional coach. The main theme of the site is career coaching for professionals and business leaders. It has also a bookstore and links to resources.

Work Zone (http://www.workzone.net)
This site is designed to help job-hunters prepare their résumés and design effective job strategies; it also offers guidelines for meaningful employment or changing careers.

3. LEARNING AND SKILLS DEVELOPMENT LINKS

CATALIST (http://prometheus.cc.uregina.ca/catalist)
Scope: Canada
The Canadian Network for Third Age Learning (CATALIST) is a bilingual network of organizations. It fosters third age learning through sharing knowledge, expertise, research and resources. A membership fee is charged for full access to the site.

Computer Skills (http://www.seniornet.org)
Scope: U.S.A. (Canadian membership accepted)
SeniorNet is a non-profit organization of 39,000 computer-using adults aged 50 and older. The organization publishes a quarterly newsletter and a variety of instructional materials; has more than 220 Learning Centers throughout the U.S.A.; offers discounts on computer-related and other products and services; holds regional conferences and collaborates in research on older adults and technology. SeniorNet operates SeniorNet Online on America

Online (keyword: SeniorNet) and on the Internet at the address shown above. The site offers hundreds of discussion topics called SeniorNet RoundTables.

Degrees for Nontraditional Students
(http://www.tradionaldegrees.com/seniors.html)
Scope: U.S.A.
This site offers a number of links to colleges and universities throughout the U.S.A. with learning programs for adults and seniors. There are also links to books on higher education for adult students.

Discovery Online (http://www.discovery.com)
Scope: U.S.A. and international
Discovery Networks, U.S. is a provider of real-world media and entertainment, offering a mix of compelling stories, high-end production values and vivid cinematography. It produces 2,100 hours of original programming each year and reaches almost 80 million households.

Eldercollege at Capilano College
(http://www.capcollege.bc.ca/continuinged/elder/index.htm)
Scope: Canada (British Columbia)
Eldercollege provides learning opportunities for older adults who wish to participate in self-directed education to contribute to the social and cultural development of their community.

Elderhostel (http://www.elderhostel.org)
Scope: U.S.A, Canada and international
Elderhostel is the United States' first and the world's largest educational and travel organization for adults 55 and over. Elderhostel has more than 12,000 programs each year in more than 100 countries.

ElderWeb (http://www.elderweb.org)
Scope: Canada and U.S.A.
ElderWeb is an online community of older adult computer users. Founded in 1994 by the Arts and Science Division of Grant MacEwan College in Edmonton, ElderWeb is designed to provide its services to all adults over 45 years of age in North America. This is a very interactive site.

Healthy Aging through Making Music (http://www.keepingthebeat.com/)
The site promotes the beneficial influence of music and music creation upon the adult mind and spirit. Includes useful links for adults who love music.

Hollyhock (http://www.hollyhock.bc.ca/)
Scope: U.S.A and Canada
Hollyhock, a holistic centre/institute, introduces itself as "an intentional centre for cultivation of human consciousness, well-being, and social impact." The site shows the programs and workshops available by topic, and details holiday offerings such as retreats and vacation arrangements. Requests for registration, for a catalogue or for an eNewsletter can be made through this site.

Institutes for Learning in Retirement (Abroad)
(http://www.eckerd.edu/aspec/ein/ilr_abroad.html)
Scope: International
The site offers a list of institutes for learning in retirement.

McGill Institute for Learning in Retirement
(http://www.mcgill.ca/conted/departments/institute)
Scope: Canada (Quebec)
The McGill Institute for Learning in Retirement (MILR) is a volunteer organization under the aegis of the Centre for Continuing Education of McGill University. Students enjoy full access to libraries and other university facilities.

Minerva Senior Studies Institute (http://www.minerva.macewan.ca)
Scope: Canada (Alberta)
Located in Edmonton, Minerva Senior Studies Institute addresses students aged 50 and older. The Institute offers more than 100 non-credit courses and workshops each year, both on and off campus, on subjects ranging from astronomy and anthropology to computers and creative writing.

National Park Service (http://www.nps.gov/)
Scope: U.S.A.
The site promotes learning about U.S. history. Some of the topics mentioned are: archeology, architecture and engineering, historic buildings and structures, museums and collections, military history, publications, travel, and history in the parks. Learning options are offered by subject and by method of

learning (for example, databases, questions and answers, lesson plans, virtual tours). This site is very easy to use thanks to a structured site map and a search engine offered on the home page.

Okanagan Institute for Learning in Retirement (http://oilr.silk.net)
Scope: Canada (British Columbia)
OILR was founded in Kelowna in 1994 by Fred Miles, a former president of the Learning in Retirement group at McGill University in Montreal, with the cooperation of the Administration and Continuing Education Department of Okanagan University College in Kelowna, British Columbia. The site offers a listing with descriptions of the courses offered.

Omega Institute (http://www.omega-inst.org)
Scope: U.S.A and international
Omega Institute promotes a holistic approach to health. It offers professional courses for becoming a counsellor, nurse, massage therapist, music therapist, etc. Workshops and conferences are also organized by Omega Institute and are accessible to all members.

Open Learning Agency (http://www.ola.bc.ca)
Scope: Canada and international
OLA is an internationally recognized leader in the delivery of lifelong learning opportunities, the development of instructional materials, and the educational use of technology in the provision of education and training services. It offers fully accredited college- and university-level courses. Flexible learning options are offered.

Points of View (http://www.pointsofviewinc.com)
The site is focused on nurturing intergenerational dialogue through training, consultation, books, tapes and motivational speaking.

Public Broadcasting Online—PBS (http://www.pbs.org)
Scope: U.S.A.
PBS Online is part of the PBS Interactive division of the Public Broadcasting Service in Alexandria, VA. PBS Online operates as a business within PBS's non-profit mission of advancing education, culture and citizenship. This site hosts more than 450 PBS television programs and specials, as well as original

Web content and real-time learning adventures. With more than 135,000 pages of content to explore, visitors can delve further into the subjects they most enjoy—from news to history and the arts to science and technology. PBS Online furthers the public broadcasting commitment to lifelong learning through super-sites such as PBS Kids, PBS TeacherSource, and The Adult Learning Service.

Routes to Learning Canada
(http://www.routestolearning.ca/home.html)
Routes to Learning Canada is a not-for-profit, charitable organization developing and coordinating educational travel programs for Canadians and visitors to Canada. Formerly ELDERHOSTEL Canada, Routes to Learning Canada continues to strengthen the bonds between Canadians and their heritage, while sharing that knowledge of Canadians with friends and visitors. A list of courses is provided as well.

School for the Second Half of Life
(http://www.exed.hbs.edu/programs/ody/index.html)
Scope: U.S.A. and international
This is a page on the Harvard Business School. HBS offers Executive Education Programs including Odyssey: School for the Second Half of Life. Odyssey is intended for professionals in the 45 to 65 age range wishing to explore the themes of change, renewal, and fulfillment in their career and their lives. Odyssey has included professionals from diverse industries and sectors and from all over the world.

Senior Net (http://www.seniornet.org/php)
The site provides adults aged 50 and over with access to education about computer technology and the Internet to enhance their lives and enable them to share their knowledge and wisdom. It is a very interactive site.

4. LIVING/BEING WELL LINKS

Ageless Beauty (http://www.beautybeyond50.com)
This site aims to influence how we age by promoting a healthy lifestyle and attitude. The information is targeted to women over or under 50 who may have anxieties about getting older or who aspire to grow old gracefully.

Alternative Medicine (http://www.alternativemedicine.com)
Alternative Medicine is a comprehensive site structured around large topics such as therapies, practitioners' yellow pages, clinics, products, remedies, books and publications. It also has a section devoted to pets.

American Council on Exercise (http://www.acefitness.org)
The American Council on Exercise® (ACE®) is a nonprofit organization committed to promoting active, healthy lifestyles and their positive effects on the mind, body and spirit. The ACE Web site is a resource for people interested in information about safe and effective exercise. It provides a search engine for finding health clubs in the U.S.A., Canada and other countries.

American Hiking Society (http://www.americanhiking.org)
American Hiking is a U.S. organization dedicated to serving hikers and protecting the nation's hiking trails. The site is rich in providing volunteer opportunities, information on hiking clubs, news, activities, policies, products, jobs and internships, and useful links related to hiking.

Ask Dr. Weil (http://www.drweil.com/app/cda/drw_cda.php)
This site focuses on wellness and health through proper diet, herbal medicines, and therapies. It offers a self-help approach to living a balanced, healthy lifestyle. A free weekly wellness bulletin is also offered.

Best Doctors (http://www.bestdoctors.com/en/default.htm)
The site provides access in both English and Spanish. Best Doctors' mission is to link consumers to the medical knowledge they need to make health care choices. The site provides health resources, summaries of a long list of medical conditions, and a directory of doctors in the U.S.A., Canada and Europe. Doctors in Canada, for instance, can be found using the AcuMatch™ database available on this site.

Breast Cancer Net (http://www.breastcancer.net)
The site provides a newsroom, support services, articles, treatment information and useful links.

Cohousing Network (http://www.cohousing.org)
Scope: U.S.A., Canada and international
The site has a list of co-housing communities, classified ads, news and events, and useful publications.

Cohousing's Cousin (http://www.neighbornets.org)
Scope: U.S.A. and Canada (British Columbia)
"Neighbornets" are affinity groups of people who live in the same general neighbourhood who choose to form closer bonds with one another. The form and organizational structure (if any) of "neighbornets" may vary widely but they are always based on sharing something—for example, time and friendships, interests and activities, skills and labour, or values.

Dietitians of Canada (http://www.dietitians.ca)
This bilingual site promotes better health through food and nutrition.

Elder Care Giving (http://www.caregiving.com)
Scope: U.S.A. and Canada
The site is devoted to care givers, with a support centre, publications, philosophy, and journals of caregivers. It also has educational materials for health care and human resources professionals.

Fellowship of Intentional Communities (http://www.ic.org)
Scope: North America
Intentional communities include eco-villages, co-housing, residential land trusts, communes, student co-ops, urban housing cooperatives and other related projects. There are more than 600 intentional communities throughout North America. The site provides a board for people seeking appropriate communities. Links to publications are also available.

Frugal Lifestyle (http://www.frugalgazette.com)
The Frugal Gazette is targeted to those wanting to get the most for every dollar they spend. The monthly newsletter, available by subscription, suggests ways to cut living expenses using simple tips and techniques. The site has a link to Free Stuff™ that provides an array of links to sites offering freebies.

Great Outdoor Recreation (http://www.gorp.com)
The site is intended for those looking for exciting trips both on the North American continent and throughout the world. There is a search engine offering the possibility of finding "the world's best active vacations." Links to publications, books and tips are also available. Membership is free.

Harvard Health Online (http://www.health.harvard.edu)
This is the site of Harvard Health Publications. It offers information from the doctors of Harvard Medical School to help users to stay healthy.

Health & Nutrition Letter—Tufts University (http://www.healthletter.tufts.edu)
This publication of Tufts University requires paid subscription. The site provides a shopping cart for nutrition books, free articles and FAQs.

Healthcare (http://www.achoo.com/main.asp)
This site helps users to locate medical information and/or citations by providing access to Medline (offers access to 9 million citations), the *Merck Manual,* and the Internet. The site allows topical searches. News and interactive communication is also possible.

Healthy Outlook (http://www.yourhealth.com)
YourHealth.com comes from McKesson Health Solutions, LLC of McKesson, Inc., a large supply management and health care information technology company. YourHealth.com and its sister brands, Personal Health Advisor® Online (PHA Online) and CareEnhance® Online, form a group of health information Web sites that are offered through health plans, employer groups, health care providers and retailers.

Home Exchanges (http://www.digsville.com)
This site offers opportunities for home and hospitality exchanges as vacation alternatives. Membership is required.

Integral Transformative Practice (http://www.itp-life.com)
Integral transformative practice is about a long-term program for realizing the potential of body, mind, heart and soul. The site provides listings with books on the topic and workshops available now and in the future; the opportunity to post personal views is also offered.

International Living (http://www.internationalliving.com)
The purpose of this site is to map the best places to live in terms of living standards and comparative cost of living. Subscription is required.

Inward Bound (http://www.inwardboundadventures.com)
Inward Bound combines yoga, NIA (neuro-integrated action), Pilates and meditation in a holistic health program. It aims to foster rejuvenation, challenge and inner peace, in settings of natural beauty.

Kripalu Center for Yoga and Health
(http://www.kripalushop.org/kripalu)
Kripalu is the largest centre for yoga and holistic health in the U.S.A, serving people of all backgrounds for more than 20 years. The educational programs offered are designed to provide participants with tools they can apply in their daily lives to foster their long-term growth and development.

Mayo Clinic (http://www.mayohealth.org/home)
This site offers search engines that may be used to locate information about diseases and conditions, drugs, and healthy living centres, as well as self-care guides, publications and news.
Neatwomen Inc. (http://www.neatwomeninc.com)
Neatwomen Inc. is for all women, but is especially targeted to women "between the ages of 45 and 105" looking for information, inspiration and motivation.

Om Page (http://www.vancouveryoga.com/home.html)
The site is addressed both to those who practice yoga and to those who teach it. It includes a search engine for yoga centres throughout Greater Vancouver.

Over the Hill Gang—Skiers 50+ (http://www.skiersover50.com)
Scope: U.S.A. and international
Over the Hill Gang offers free membership for everybody from 50 years old onward. Membership benefits include discounts. There is an online yearly catalogue of trips. Press releases are also available.

Relocating (http://www.bestplaces.net)
Scope: U.S.A.
In 1985, Bert Sperling developed a software program named "Places, U.S.A." which allowed people to enter their personal preferences to find their "best place." While it is limited to U.S. cities and towns, it provides some guidance on factors to consider when selecting a place to live.

Seniors and Spirituality (http://www.senioradultministry.com)
The Association for Lifelong Adult Ministry is dedicated to serving those who work with, or seek to work with, adults in the second half of life. The site provides a link to Johnson Institute, which offers courses related to adult spiritual development.

Shape Up America! (http://www.shapeup.org)
This site intends to help Americans moderate their body fat through balanced nutrition, fitness and lifestyle. The site also provides a link for health professionals.

Simple Living Network (http://www.simpleliving.net)
The Simple Living Network is a small home-based business that provides information about resources and free community services that may help users live a simpler lifestyle.

Snowbirds (http://www.snowbirdhelper.com/canadian_links.htm)
Canadian Snowbirds are a big part of the U.S. Snowbird scene. The site is meant to provide information that will be helpful while in the U.S.A. or when planning a trip. The goal of this site is to help all Canadians feel at home while in the U.S.A.

WebMD—Health (http://my.webmd.com)
This comprehensive site offers links to information about diseases and conditions, healthy lifestyle, parenting and pregnancy, drugs and herbs, sports and fitness, communities, e-commerce and so on.

Wellness (http://www.50plus.org)
Fifty-Plus is an international organization devoted to information about, motivation towards, and participation in exercise and fitness while aging.

Wired Seniors (http://www.wiredseniors.com/ageofreason)
This site addresses people over 50 who seek information but don't want to inhabit "Never Ending Cyberspace." Practical information relevant to seniors' lifestyles is plentifully supplied.

Yoga Basics (http://www.yogabasics.com)
This site provides an online guide to hatha yoga, including the history and philosophy of the yogic path, a visual guide to the postures of yoga, and an extensive yoga resource guide.

Yoga Site (http://www.yogasite.com)
The site is structured around the following topics: teacher directory (U.S.), yoga postures, yoga retreats, yoga styles, yoga therapy news, meditations, yoga organizations and yoga news groups.

5. WORTH VISITING

AARP (http://www.aarp.org/)
Scope: U.S.A. (membership is accepted from Canadians)
The AARP Foundation administers educational, employment and community service programs funded by nearly $55 million from both federal and private sources. Its purpose is to support public education, advocacy and community service activities in states and communities. AARP works in both the private and the public sectors to improve the quality of life for its members and for all U.S. citizens as they grow older. Topics covered on this site are: computers and technology, health and wellness, learning, legislation and elections, life answers, money and work, policy and research, travel and leisure, and volunteering. The site offers links to AARP publications and magazines as well as to AgeLine, a searchable electronic database containing more than 60,000 abstracts on current literature on aging. This database is useful both for the general public and for professionals and researchers.

CARP (Canada's Association for the Fifty-Plus) (http://www.50plus.com)
Scope: Canada
CARP stands for Canadian Association of Retired Persons. This name no longer describes CARP's members, who are 50 years or older, retired or not—hence the new descriptor. This is a comprehensive site and very interactive for its members. It approaches most of the large topics of interest for the 50+

generations. Among the large topics are health, travel, entertainment and business.

Consciousness Research (http://www.noetic.org)
This is the site of the Institute of Noetic Sciences (IONS) in California. It is a non-profit organization that both conducts and sponsors research into the workings and powers of the mind, including perceptions, beliefs, attention, intention, and intuition. The site's offerings include publications and a list of IONS-sponsored events.

50plus! Online (http://www.fifty-plus.com/about.html)
50plus! is a Cincinnati-based health and lifestyle initiative featuring an editorially driven monthly newspaper and an interactive Web site. The site features selected articles from the print newspaper, and an Internet directory. The site also has easy-to-use links to other Web sites and search engines, making Web surfing simple and informative.

iGrandparents.com (http://www.igrandparents.com/default.asp)
There is a large array of links structured around topics such as: antiques, history, health and fitness, games, newspapers and free products. The site is interactive, providing chat rooms, tours and so on.

Just What I Asked For (http://www.jwiaf.com)
This is an Internet directory aimed at making it easier to find quality resources on the Internet. Topics are arranged under broad headings with hyperlinks connecting to listings of Web sites on each subject.

Longevity Research (http://www.longevityworld.com)
The site emphasizes a few subjects related to longevity: spirituality, think tanks, poetry of life transitions.

Senior Lifestyle (http://www.senior-lifestyle.com)
Senior Lifestyle is the Web version of *Senior Lifestyle Magazine*, which focuses mostly on people 50 and older.

Senior Spirit: An E-zine for 50+ Women (http://senior-spirit.com)
The site includes topics on lifestyle, health, diet, fashion and travel; a bookstore; "grandma's guide," etc. It provides a forum and a plethora of useful links for senior women.

Senior Women Web (http://www.seniorwomen.com)
This site addresses women in their 50+ years and covers an array of interests such as: culture and arts, money and computing, employment, entertaining, home and shopping, news, health, life styles, travel and grandparenting. The site has a discussion forum and a search engine.

Suddenly Senior (http://www.suddenlysenior.com)
Suddenly Senior offers stories of real-life experiences to touch both the heart and the funny bone.

Third Age (http://www.thirdage.com)
This very interactive site provides chat, discussions, free classes, e-mail tools and games. Topics include beauty and style, computers, health, horoscope, money and travel.

Wundercodger (http://www.wundercodger.com)
The site offers a free community forum, resources pages, tips and tools for locating people, links to recommended shopping sites, humour, poetry, interviews and so on. Worth a visit for its lighthearted approach!